EVENING PRAYER
FOR SUNDAYS

Vespers from *The Divine Office*

In the same series

NIGHT PRAYER
Compline from *The Divine Office*

EVENING PRAYER FOR SUNDAYS

Vespers from
The Divine Office

COLLINS

First published 1975

Taken from *The Divine Office*, a translation of *Liturgia
Horarum*, approved by the Episcopal Conferences of
Australia, England and Wales, Ireland, Scotland. Also
approved for use in Gambia, Ghana, India, Kenya, Liberia,
Malaysia and Singapore, New Zealand, Nigeria, Rhodesia,
Sierra Leone, Tanzania, Uganda.

The publishers gratefully acknowledge the co-operation
of the Diocese of Southwark Commission for the Liturgy
in the planning of this work.

**Cum originali concordat: John P. Dewis
Imprimatur: David Norris
3 April 1975**

ISBN 0 00 599525 6 (limp cover)
ISBN 0 00 599534 5 (cased)
Set in Monotype Plantin
Made and printed in Great Britain by
William Collins Sons & Co Ltd, Glasgow

CONTENTS

THE CELEBRATION OF EVENING PRAYER

The Divine Office

Evening Prayer, or Vespers as it used to be called, is part of *The Divine Office*, the official prayer of the Church, the Liturgy of the Hours. In this prayer, the Church offers prayer and praise to the Father at all times, so as to consecrate every hour of the day and night. This prayer is not a private function, and not the property of the clergy and religious who are nevertheless obliged to pray it each day. It belongs to the whole body of the Church, and as far as possible, it should be celebrated with the people taking part.

In this body, the parishes which could be called the cells of the diocese, are most important, and wherever possible, Evening Prayer and Morning Prayer should be celebrated in common at the local church. Wherever groups of the laity are gathered and whatever the reason which has brought them together, such as prayer or the apostolate, they are encouraged to recite the Church's Office by celebrating part of the Liturgy of the Hours. And it is fitting that the family, which is the domestic sanctuary of the Church, should also say certain parts of the Liturgy of the Hours, in this way uniting themselves more closely to the Church.

Evening Prayer

Evening Prayer is celebrated when the day is drawing to a close, so that we may give thanks for what has been given us during the day, or for the things we have done well during it (St Basil). At Evening Prayer we call to mind our redemption, through the prayer we offer "like incense in the sight of the Lord", in which "the raising up of our hands" becomes "an evening sacrifice" (Psalm 140:2).

The parts of Evening Prayer

1. The prayer opens with the introductory verse *O God, come to our aid: O Lord, make haste to help us,* followed by the *Glory be to the Father,* and (except in Lent) *Alleluia.*

2. A hymn follows, to open the celebration and express the theme of the feast or season, and of the time of day. A small number of hymns from *The Divine Office* is given in the appendix to this

volume. Any other suitable hymn may be chosen from *The Divine Office*, or from hymns approved by the Episcopal Conference. (In practice this means that a hymn suitable for Evening Prayer and for the season may be chosen from a recognised hymn book.)

3. The psalmody follows. The Church prays with the beautiful songs composed under the Spirit of God by the sacred authors of the Old Testament. The psalms are the backbone of the Divine Office, and of Christian prayer down through the centuries. They express the pain and hope, misery and confidence of men of every age and land, and especially sing of faith in God, his revelation and redemption.

Even if the mood of the psalm does not accord with one's own feelings at the time one is praying it, one can and should pray the psalm with and for the Church: whoever prays the psalms in the Liturgy of the Hours does not say them in his own name so much as in the name of the whole body of Christ, in fact in the person of Christ himself.

At Evening Prayer, there are always two psalms (or a longer psalm may be divided into two parts), followed by a canticle of praise from the New Testament. Psalms and canticle always end with the *Glory be to the Father*.

Antiphons: each psalm and canticle has its own antiphon, which is said or sung before and after the psalm, providing a special "colour" or theme for the psalm.

5. Scripture Reading. The proclamation of the Word of God is an essential element of every liturgical celebration. A short reading is given with each Evening Prayer. A longer reading may be substituted for this, chosen from the Office of Readings for the day, or from the Lectionary, or any other suitable reading may be chosen. The Gospels, however, are not used in the Divine Office (except in Vigils) since they are read in their entirety each year at Mass.

6. A homily may be preached, reflecting on the scripture reading. A period of silence may follow it.

7. Short Responsory: this acts as a reflection on, and response to, the word of God. It may be sung, or said. It may be omitted.

The manner of saying it, in communal celebration, is for the cantor or reader to announce the response, which the people repeat; the cantor says the verse, the people repeat the response; the cantor says the first half of the *Glory be to the Father*, and all together repeat the response. (In the offices for the Sundays of the Year, given below, the short responsory is set out fully in this way.)

In private recitation, the repeated parts may be omitted.

8. The *Magnificat*, the Canticle of the Blessed Virgin Mary (Luke 1:46-55) is sung or said. Its antiphon is repeated before and after the canticle. The same honour is accorded to this Canticle as to the Gospel. All stand during its recitation.

9. The Intercessions are directed immediately to God. The priest or minister introduces them with a short invitation. Each intention consists of two parts, the second of which may be used as a variable response. Alternatively, the people may reply to the intention by using the simple response, or pause for silence after each intention.

Further intentions may be added for the needs of the Church, the world, or the local community, but the last intercession at Evening Prayer is always the one given for the dead.

At the end of the Intercessions, all say together the Lord's Prayer, and the concluding prayer of the day is said by the priest or minister.

10. Conclusion: the blessing and dismissal are given by the priest as at Mass. If no priest or deacon is present, a simple form of dismissal is used

11. Silence: in order to allow the voice of the Holy Spirit to be heard more fully in our hearts, and to unite our personal prayer more closely with the word of God and the public voice of the Church, opportunity for silence should be given in the recitation of Evening Prayer.

Celebration of Evening Prayer with Mass or Exposition of the Blessed Sacrament

The norms for celebrating Evening Prayer with Mass will be found in the General Instruction on the Liturgy of the Hours, 94, 96, 97.

Evening Prayer may be celebrated before the Blessed Sacrament exposed, when there is a lengthy period of exposition. After ex-

position of the Blessed Sacrament in the usual way and a pause for
silent prayer, the Office begins with the hymn or directly with the
antiphons and psalms. After the concluding prayer, the conclusion
of the hour is omitted, and Benediction with the Blessed Sacrament is given.

Celebrating Evening Prayer

If a priest or deacon is present, he will lead the celebration; if it
takes place in a church, he will do so from the sanctuary. Otherwise,
a suitable religious or lay person is appointed as prayer leader, and
will lead the celebration from outside the sanctuary. A lector should
read the scripture reading, and the short responsory if it is not sung.

If there is no singing, the leader, or an antiphoner, may lead the
antiphons and psalms; if there is singing, one or more cantors will
lead antiphons, psalms and short responsory. An organist or other
instrumentalist will then be useful, and possibly singers among the
congregation to lead its singing. Altar servers will enhance solemn
celebrations: acolytes, thurifer and MC.

All taking part stand:
   a. during the introduction to the Hour
   b. during the hymn
   c. during the Gospel canticle
   d. during intercessions, Lord's Prayer, concluding prayer
During the psalms and canticles, those present may sit or stand,
according to custom. All sit during the reading.

All make the sign of the cross during the introductory verse, and
at the beginning of the Magnificat.

> (Abridged from *General Instruction*, passim.)

The following is a description of a solemn celebration of Evening
Prayer. All details may be simplified, or elaborated.

The presiding priest vests in alb, stole and cope of the liturgical
colour of the day. At the appointed time, he proceeds to the
sanctuary, preceded by two acolytes with lighted candles, the
thurifer (without thurible) and the MC. The people stand. After the
customary reverence, the acolytes place their candles at or near the
altar; the priest goes to the chair, where he says or sings *O God,*

come to our aid. All make the sign of the cross, and say the response, adding the *Glory be to the Father* and (except in Lent) *Alleluia.* All sing the hymn, and then sit. The antiphoner or cantor leads the saying or singing of the antiphon: if the people do not know the melody of the antiphon, it may be sung by the choir, or it may be said, even if the psalms will be sung.

The psalm and canticle may be sung or said as follows: one or two cantors or the antiphoner may sing or say verses alternately with the congregation, or two parts of the congregation (e.g. opposite sides of the church) may alternate the verses. Each "side" should have adequate vocal strength. Unless the music requires otherwise, it is recommended that verses should be alternated as printed. Each psalm and canticle ends with the *Glory be to the Father,* and then the antiphon is repeated.

All remain seated during the antiphons, psalms and canticle, except for the cantor(s) and antiphoner who may stand to begin an antiphon or psalm. All remain seated also for the reading, the homily, the silence, and short responsory (if included). The lector proclaims the reading from the lectern or other suitable place. The thurifer prepares the thurible in time for the Magnificat.

All stand. The Magnificat antiphon is sung or said. The priest or cantor begins the Magnificat and all make the sign of the cross. This canticle may be sung or said in the manner of the psalms, or everyone may sing or say it throughout. The priest puts incense in the thurible at the chair and then moves to incense the cross and the altar, as for Mass. He returns to the chair, where he is incensed by the MC or thurifer, who then incenses the congregation. The *Glory be to the Father* at the end of the Magnificat is not sung or said until the incensation is complete. The Magnificat antiphon is repeated and all remain standing for the intercessions, the Lord's Prayer, and the concluding prayer, which are led by the priest from the chair. The response at the intercession may be announced beforehand. It may be sung, in which case the people may repeat it each time after the cantor. The priest may greet the people after the concluding prayer, and make any necessary announcements. The blessing is given from the chair, the acolytes pick up their candles, and priest and ministers return to the sacristy.

THE ORDER OF EVENING PRAYER

Introduction
℣ O God, come to our aid.
℟ **O Lord, make haste to help us.**
Glory be to the Father and to the Son and to the Holy Spirit, as it
was in the beginning, is now, and ever shall be, world without end.
Amen. Alleluia.
The alleluia is not said during Lent.

Hymn
This varies according to the Season of the Year, or the Feast.

Psalmody
*The antiphons and Psalms vary according to the Season of the Year,
or the Feast. The Order is:*
    Antiphon 1   Psalm   Repeat Antiphon 1
    Antiphon 2   Psalm   Repeat Antiphon 2
    Antiphon 3   Canticle   Repeat Antiphon 3

Scripture Reading
This varies according to the Season of the Year, or the Feast.

Short Responsory
This varies according to the Season of the Year, or the Feast.

The Canticle of Mary (Magnificat)   *Luke 1:45-55*
*Magnificat Antiphon: This varies according to the Season of the Year,
or the Feast.*

My soul glorifies the Lord,*
my spirit rejoices in God, my Saviour.
He looks on his servant in her lowliness;*
henceforth all ages will call me blessed.

The Almighty works marvels for me.*
Holy his name!
His mercy is from age to age,*
on those who fear him.

He puts forth his arm in strength*
and scatters the proud-hearted.
He casts the mighty from their thrones*
and raises the lowly.

He fills the starving with good things,*
sends the rich away empty.

He protects Israel, his servant,*
remembering his mercy,
the mercy promised to our fathers,*
to Abraham and his sons for ever.

Glory be to the Father . . .

Repeat Magnificat Antiphon.

Intercessions
These vary according to the Season of the Year, or the Feast.

The Lord's Prayer
This may be introduced in the following or similar words:
Let us now pray in the words our Saviour gave us: *Our Father . . .*

Concluding Prayer
This varies according to the Season of the Year, or the Feast.

Conclusion
When a priest or deacon presides:
The Lord be with you.   ℟ **And also with you.**
May almighty God bless you, the Father, and the Son, and the
Holy Spirit.   ℟ **Amen.**

*Another form of blessing may be used as in the Missal. The people are
then invited to leave:*
Go in the peace of Christ.   ℟ **Thanks be to God.**

*When no priest or deacon is present, or in recitation on one's own, the
conclusion is as follows:*
The Lord bless us, and keep us from all evil, and bring us to
everlasting life.   ℟ **Amen.**

THE PROPER OF SEASONS

SUNDAYS 1-4 OF ADVENT

Hymn

Psalmody

Ant. 1: Rejoice greatly, daughter of Sion, shout with gladness, daughter of Jerusalem, alleluia.
PSALM 109, NO. 2.

Ant. 2: Christ our King will come. He is the Lamb that John announced.
PSALM 113A, NO. 6.

Ant. 3: Behold I am coming soon to reward every man according to his deed, says the Lord.
CANTICLE, CF REVELATION 19:1-2, 5-7, NO. 21.

Ant. 1: Behold, the Lord will come on the clouds of heaven with great strength, alleluia.
PSALM 109, NO. 2.

Ant. 2: The Lord will come and will not disappoint us. Wait for him if he seems to delay, for he will surely come, alleluia.
PSALM 113B, NO. 7.

Ant. 3: The Lord is our judge, the Lord is our King. He will come and make us whole.
CANTICLE, CF REVELATION 19:1-2, 5-7, NO. 21.

Ant. 1: See, the Lord will come. He will sit with princes and he will mount the glorious throne.
PSALM 109, NO. 2.

Ant. 2: The mountains will bring forth joy and the hills justice; for the Lord, the light of the world, comes in strength.
PSALM 110, NO. 3.

Ant. 3: Let us live justly and honestly while we are awaiting, in hope, the coming of the Lord.
CANTICLE, CF REVELATION 19:1-2, 5-7, NO. 21.

SUNDAY 4
Ant. 1: See, how splendid is he who comes to save the peoples.
PSALM 109, NO. 2.

Ant. 2: The rugged places shall be made smooth and the mountain-ranges shall become plains. Come, Lord, and do not delay, alleluia.
PSALM 111, NO. 4.

Ant. 3: Great will be his reign and peace will be everlasting, alleluia.
CANTICLE, CF REVELATION 19:1-2, 5-7, NO. 21.

Scripture Reading   *Philippians 4:4-5*
Rejoice in the Lord always; again I will say, Rejoice. Let all men know your forbearance. The Lord is at hand.

Short Responsory
℟ Show us, Lord, your steadfast love. *Repeat* ℟
℣ And grant us your salvation. ℟ Glory be. ℟

Magnificat Antiphon
Sunday 1: Do not be afraid, Mary, for you have found favour with God. Behold, you will conceive and bear a son, alleluia.

Sunday 2: Blessed are you, Mary, because you had faith: the Lord's promise to you will be fulfilled, alleluia.

Sunday 3: "Are you the one who is to come, or are we to expect another?" "Tell John what you hear and see: the blind see again, the lame walk, and the good news is preached to those who are poor in spirit, alleluia."

Sunday 4: as for 17 to 23 December, pp. 17-18.

Intercessions

We pray to our Lord, who is the way, the truth, and the life.

℞ **Come, and remain with us, Lord.**

Gabriel announced your coming to the Virgin Mary:
—Son of the Most High, come to claim your kingdom. ℞

John the Baptist rejoiced to see your day:—come, bring us your salvation. ℞

Simeon acknowledged you, Light of the World:—bring your light to all men of goodwill. ℞

We look for you as watchmen look for the dawn:—you are the sun that will wake the dead to new life. ℞

Our Father

The voice of John crying in the wilderness is echoed tonight in the voice of the Church:

℞ **Make our hearts ready, O Lord!**

For your coming to us in grace this Advent, —℞

For the work man must do in creating a more just world, —℞

For the understanding we shall need this week for our families and friends, —℞

For our death, for our judgement, for eternal life with you, —℞

Our Father

Concluding Prayer

Sunday 1: Grant, almighty Father,
that when Christ comes again
we may go out to meet him,
bearing the harvest of good works
achieved by your grace.
We pray that he will receive us into the company of the saints
and call us into the kingdom of heaven.
(We make our prayer) through our Lord.

Sunday 2: Almighty and merciful God,
let neither our daily work nor the cares of this life
prevent us from hastening to meet your Son.

Enlighten us with your wisdom
and lead us into his company.
(We make our prayer) through our Lord.

Sunday 3: Grant, almighty God, that looking forward in faith
to the feast of our Lord's birth,
we may feel all the happiness our Saviour brings,
and celebrate his coming with unfailing joy.
(We make our prayer) through our Lord.

Sunday 4: Lord, open our hearts to your grace.
Through the angel's message to Mary
we have learned to believe
in the incarnation of Christ your Son.
Lead us by his passion and cross
to the glory of his resurrection.
(We make our prayer) through our Lord.

MAGNIFICAT ANTIPHONS
17-23 December

17 December: O Wisdom, you come forth from the mouth of the
Most High. You fill the universe and hold all things together in a
strong yet gentle manner. O come to teach us the way of truth.

18 December: O Adonai and leader of Israel, you appeared to Moses
in a burning bush and you gave him the Law on Sinai. O come and
save us with your mighty power.

19 December: O stock of Jesse, you stand as a signal for the nations;
kings fall silent before you whom the peoples acclaim. O come to
deliver us, and do not delay.

20 December: O key of David and sceptre of Israel, what you open
no one else can close again; what you close no one can open. O
come to lead the captive from prison; free those who sit in darkness
and in the shadow of death.

E.P.S.

21 December: O Rising Sun, you are the splendour of eternal light and the sun of justice. O come and enlighten those who sit in darkness and in the shadow of death.

22 December: O King whom all the peoples desire, you are the cornerstone which makes all one. O come and save man whom you made from clay.

23 December: O Immanuel, you are our king and judge, the One whom the peoples await and their Saviour. O come and save us, Lord, our God.

CHRISTMAS EVE

Hymn

Psalmody

Ant. 1: The King of Peace has shown himself in glory: all the peoples desire to see him.

PSALM 112, NO. 5.

Ant. 2: He sends out his word to the earth and swiftly runs his command.

PSALM 147, NO. 14.

Ant. 3: The Word of God, born of the Father before time began, humbled himself today for us and became man.

CANTICLE, PHILIPPIANS 2:6-11, NO. 16.

Scripture Reading   *Galatians 4:4-5*

When the appointed time came, God sent his Son, born of a woman, —born a subject of the Law, to redeem the subjects of the Law and to enable us to be adopted as sons.

Short Responsory

R̝ Today you know that the Lord will come. *Repeat* R̝
V̝ In the morning you will see his glory. R̝ Glory be. R̝

Magnificat ant. When the sun rises in the heavens you will see the king of kings. He comes forth from the Father like a bridegroom coming in splendour from his wedding chamber.

Intercessions
Let us turn in prayer to Christ who emptied himself to assume the
condition of a slave. He was tempted in every way that we are, but
did not sin.

℟ **Save us through your birth.**
Coming into our world, Lord Jesus, you open the new age which
the prophets foretold. —In every age, may the Church come again
to new birth. ℟
You took on our human weakness.—Be the eyes of the blind, the
strength of the weak, the friend of the lonely. ℟
Lord, you were born among the poor:—show them your love. ℟
Your birth brings eternal life within man's reach;—comfort the
dying with hope of new life in heaven. ℟
Gather the departed to yourself;—and make them radiant in your
glory. ℟
Our Father

Concluding Prayer
Fill us with confidence, Lord God,
when your Only-begotten Son comes as our judge.
We welcome him with joy as our redeemer;
year by year renew that joy
as we await the fulfilment of our redemption
by Jesus Christ our Lord, your Son,
who lives and reigns with you and the Holy Spirit,
God, for ever and ever.

CHRISTMAS DAY

Hymn

Psalmody
Ant. 1: All authority and dominion are yours on the day of your
strength; you are resplendent in holiness. From the womb before
the dawn I begot you.
PSALM 109, NO. 2.

Ant. 2: With the Lord there is unfailing love. Great is his power to set men free.
PSALM 129, NO. 12.

Ant. 3: The word was God in the beginning and before all times; today he is born to us, the Saviour of the world.
CANTICLE, COLOSSIANS 1:12-20, NO. 17.

Scripture Reading   *1 John 1:1-3*
Something which has existed since the beginning,
that we have heard,
and we have seen with our own eyes;
that we have watched
and touched with our hands:
the Word, who is life—
this is our subject.
That life was made visible:
we saw it and we are giving our testimony,
telling you of the eternal life
which was with the Father
and has been made visible to us.
What we have seen and heard
we are telling you
so that you too may be in union with us,
as we are in union
with the Father
and with his Son Jesus Christ.

Short Responsory
℞ The Word became flesh, alleluia, alleluia. *Repeat* ℞
℣ And he lived among us. ℞ Glory be. ℞

Magnificat ant. Today Christ is born, today the Saviour has appeared; today the angels sing on earth, the archangels rejoice; today upright men shout out for joy: Glory be to God on high, alleluia.

Intercessions
Today the angels' message rings through the world. Gathered

together in prayer, we rejoice in the birth of our brother, the Saviour of us all. ℟ **Lord Jesus, your birth is our peace.**

May our lives express what we celebrate at Christmas:—may its mystery enrich your Church this year. ℟

We join the shepherds in adoring you,—we kneel before you, holy child of Bethlehem. ℟

We pray for the shepherds of your Church:—be close to them as they proclaim your birth to mankind. ℟

As we travel on this earthly pilgrimage, may your light shine in our hearts,—and may we see your glory, born in our midst. ℟

Word of the Father, you became man for us and raised us to a new life.—May the dead share with us in the new birth which Christmas proclaims. ℟

Our Father

Concluding Prayer
God, our Father,
our human nature is the wonderful work of your hands,
made still more wonderful by your work of redemption.
Your Son took to himself our manhood,
grant us a share in the godhead of Jesus Christ,
who lives and reigns with you and the Holy Spirit,
God, for ever and ever.

Sunday within the Octave of Christmas
THE HOLY FAMILY

Feast

Hymn

Psalmody
Ant. 1: After three days they found Jesus in the Temple, sitting among the doctors, listening to them and asking them questions.
PSALM 121, NO. 10.

Ant. 2: Jesus went down with them to Nazareth and lived under their authority.
PSALM 126, NO. 11.

Ant. 3: As Jesus grew up, he advanced in wisdom and favour with God and men.
CANTICLE, EPHESIANS 1:3-10, NO. 15.

Scripture Reading   *Philippians 2:6-7*
In your minds you must be the same as Christ Jesus: His state was divine, yet he did not cling to his equality with God but emptied himself to assume the condition of a slave and become as men are.

Short Responsory
R̷ He had to be made like his brothers in every way, so that he might be merciful. *Repeat* R̷
V̷ He appeared on earth and lived among men. R̷ Glory be. R̷

Magnificat ant. "Son, why have you treated us like this? Your father and I have been looking for you anxiously." "Why were you looking for me? Did you not know that I was bound to be where my Father is?"

Intercessions
Let us adore the Son of the living God, who became son in a human family.
   R̷ **Lord Jesus, bless our families.**
By your obedience to Mary and Joseph, — teach us how to respect proper authority and order. R̷
By the love that filled your home, — give our families the grace of loving harmony and peace. R̷
Your first intent was the honour of your Father. — May God be the heart of all our family life. R̷
Your parents found you teaching in your Father's house. — Help us, like you, to seek first the Father's will. R̷
By your reunion with Mary and Joseph in the joy of heaven, — welcome our dead into the family of the saints. R̷
Our Father

Concluding Prayer
God, our Father,
in the Holy Family of Nazareth

you have given us the true model of a Christian home.
Grant that by following Jesus, Mary, and Joseph
in their love for each other and in the example of their family life
we may come to your home of peace and joy.
(We make our prayer) through our Lord.

1 January   Octave of Christmas
MARY, THE MOTHER OF GOD
Solemnity

Hymn

Psalmody
Ant. 1: O wonderful exchange! The Creator of human nature took on a human body and was born of the Virgin. He became man without having a human father and has bestowed on us his divine nature.
PSALM 121, NO. 10.

Ant. 2: You were born of the Virgin in a mysterious manner of which no man can speak; you fulfilled the scriptures: like rain falling gently on the earth you came hither to save the human race. We praise you; you are our God.
PSALM 126, NO. 11.

Ant. 3: Moses saw the thornbush which was on fire yet was not burnt up. In it we see a sign of your virginity which all must honour; Mother of God, pray for us.
CANTICLE, EPHESIANS 1:3-10, NO. 15.

Scripture Reading   *Galatians 4:4-5*
When the appointed time came, God sent his Son, born of a woman, born a subject of the Law, to redeem the subjects of the Law and to enable us to be adopted as sons.

Short Responsory
R̷ The Word became flesh, alleluia, alleluia. *Repeat* R̷
V̷ And he lived among us. R̷ Glory be. R̷

Magnificat ant. Blessed is the womb that bore you, Christ, and blessed are the breasts that suckled you, for you are the Lord and Saviour of the world, alleluia.

Intercessions

Blessed be Christ, Immanuel, whom the Virgin conceived and brought forth.

℞ **Son of the Virgin Mary, hear our prayer.**

You gave the Virgin Mary the joys of motherhood;—grant to all parents joy in their children. ℞

King of peace, your kingdom is one of justice and peace;—grant that we may seek those things that will further harmony among men. ℞

You came to build the human race into a holy people;—bind the nations together in the unity of the Spirit. ℞

You were born into a human family;—strengthen with love the bonds of family life. ℞

You came to a life of weakness in our world;—grant to the dead the life of glory in your kingdom. ℞

Our Father

Concluding Prayer

God, our Father,
since you gave mankind a saviour through blessed Mary,
virgin and mother,
grant that we may feel the power of her intercession
when she pleads for us with Jesus Christ, your Son,
the author of life,
who lives and reigns with you and the Holy Spirit,
God, for ever and ever.

SECOND SUNDAY AFTER CHRISTMAS

Hymn

Psalmody

Ant. 1: A new day of redemption has dawned for us. It was prepared from of old and holds the promise of eternal joy.
PSALM 109, NO. 2.

Ant. 2: The Lord has sent his mercy; he has shown his faithfulness.
PSALM 113B, NO. 7.

Ant. 3: The Lord, the King of kings, has been born for us on earth: now the salvation of the world, our redemption, has come to us, alleluia.
CANTICLE, CF REVELATION 19:1-2, 5-7, NO. 21.

Scripture Reading   *1 John 1:1-3*
Something which has existed since the beginning,
that we have heard,
and we have seen with our own eyes;
that we have watched
and touched with our hands:
the Word, who is life—
this is our subject.
That life was made visible:
we saw it and we are giving our testimony,
telling you of the eternal life
which was with the Father and has been made visible to us.
What we have seen and heard
we are telling you
so that you too may be in union with us,
as we are in union with the Father
and with his Son Jesus Christ.

Short Responsory
℟ The Word became flesh, alleluia, alleluia. *Repeat* ℟
℣ And he lived among us. ℟ Glory be. ℟

Magnificat ant. Blessed is the womb that bore the Son of the eternal Father, and blessed are the breasts that suckled Christ the Lord.

Intercessions

At Christ's birth the angels proclaimed peace to the world. Let us praise him with joy and ask his favour:

℟ **Let your birth bring peace to all men.**

Lord, fill your Church with all blessings;—strengthen her by the mystery of your birth. ℟

You came as chief shepherd and guardian of our souls;—keep the pope and the bishops faithful stewards of your grace in all its forms. ℟

Eternal King, it was your will to experience human limitations and death;—help us in our weakness and grant us a share in your eternal kingdom. ℟

You were awaited from the ages and you came in the fulness of time;—show yourself to those who still await you. ℟

In coming among us as a man you redeemed our human nature from the corruption of death;—grant to the dead the fulness of your redemption. ℟

Our Father

Concluding Prayer

Almighty, ever-living God, light of every faithful soul,
fill the world with your glory,
and reveal to all nations the splendour of your presence.
(We make our prayer) through our Lord.

6 January   or Sunday between 2 and 8 January
THE EPIPHANY OF THE LORD

Hymn

Psalmody

Ant. 1: The King of Peace is more glorious than all the kings of the world.

PSALM 109, NO. 2.

Ant. 2: A beacon now shines in the darkness for honest men; the Lord is compassionate, merciful, and kind.

PSALM III, NO. 4.

Ant. 3: All peoples, that you have made, will come and adore you, Lord.

CANTICLE, REVELATION 15:3-4, NO. 20.

Scripture Reading *Titus 3:4-5*
When the kindness and love of God our Saviour appeared, he saved us. It was not because of any good works that we ourselves had done, but because of his own mercy that he saved us through the washing by which the Holy Spirit gives us new birth and new life.

Short Responsory
R̰ All the peoples will be blessed in him. *Repeat* R̰
V̰ All nations will praise him. R̰ Glory be. R̰

Magnificat ant. Three wonders mark this day we celebrate: today the star led the Magi to the manger; today water was changed into wine at the marriage feast; today Christ desired to be baptised by John in the river Jordan to bring us salvation, alleluia.

Intercessions
Today the Magi knelt before our Saviour. Let us also worship him with great joy, and pray:
R̰ **Lord, save us in our need.**
King of nations, the wise men came from the East to worship you:
—grant us the true spirit of adoration and submission. R̰
King of glory, your people look to you for judgement:—grant an abundance of peace to our world. R̰
King of ages, your word is ever powerful:—may it penetrate our hearts and lives today. R̰
King of justice, show your love for the poor and the powerless;—strengthen those who are suffering. R̰
King of heaven, hope of all who trust in you;—give to the faithful departed the wonders of your salvation. R̰
Our Father

Concluding Prayer
On this day, Lord God,
by a guiding star you revealed your Only-begotten Son
to all the peoples of the world.
Lead us from the faith by which we know you now
to the vision of your glory, face to face.
(We make our prayer) through our Lord.

Sunday after Epiphany
THE BAPTISM OF THE LORD

Hymn

Psalmody
Ant. 1: The voice of the Father was heard from heaven: This is my
Son with whom I am well pleased; listen to his word.
PSALM 109, NO. 2.

Ant. 2: The Saviour crushed the head of the serpent in the river
Jordan; he released all men from his power.
PSALM 111, NO. 4.

Ant. 3: Today a great mystery is revealed to us: the creator of all
things released us from the bond of our sins in the river Jordan.
CANTICLE, REVELATION 15:3-4, NO. 20.

Scripture Reading   *Acts 10:37-38*
You know of the great events that took place throughout all of
Judea, beginning in Galilee, after the baptism that John preached.
You know about Jesus of Nazareth, how God poured out on him
the Holy Spirit and power. He went everywhere, doing good and
healing all who were under the power of the Devil, for God was
with him.

Short Responsory
℟ This is he who has come by water and by blood. *Repeat* ℟
℣ This is Jesus Christ, our Lord. ℟ Glory be. ℟

Magnificat ant. Jesus Christ has loved us and has purified us from our sins in his blood. He has made us a kingdom and priesthood for God and his Father. To him be glory and kingly power for ever.

Intercessions
Let us pray to our Redeemer who humbled himself to receive baptism at the hands of John.
℞. **Lord, send us your Spirit.**
Christ, servant of the Father and pleasing to him,—send forth your Spirit among us. ℞.
Chosen One of God, you did not break the crushed reed nor quench the wavering flame;—let all men know your compassion for our world of weakness. ℞.
You were anointed with the Holy Spirit to be our Saviour;—lead all men to believe in you and so come to eternal life. ℞.
You are God's light to the nations;—open the eyes of the blind in the baptismal waters of the new covenant. ℞.
You are the hope of all peoples;—receive the faithful departed into your heavenly kingdom. ℞.
Our Father

Concluding Prayer
Almighty, ever-living God,
when Christ was baptised in the river Jordan
the Holy Spirit came upon him
and your voice proclaimed from heaven "This is my beloved Son."
Grant that we,
who by water and the Holy Spirit are your adopted children,
may continue steadfast in your love.
(We make our prayer) through our Lord.

SUNDAYS 1–4 OF LENT

Hymn

Psalmody

Ant. 1: You must worship the Lord, your God, and serve him alone.
PSALM 109, NO. 2.

Ant. 2: Now is the favourable time; this is the day of salvation.
PSALM 113A, NO. 6.

Ant. 3: Now we are going up to Jerusalem, and everything that is written about the Son of Man will come true.
CANTICLE, I PETER 2:21-24, NO. 18.

SUNDAY 2
Ant. 1: The Lord will send forth your sceptre of power with the splendour of the saints.
PSALM 109, NO. 2.

Ant. 2: We worship the one God, who made heaven and earth.
PSALM 113B, NO. 7.

Ant. 3: God did not spare his own Son but gave him up for us all.
CANTICLE, I PETER 2:21-24, NO. 18.

SUNDAY 3
Ant. 1: Lord, almighty king, deliver us for the sake of your name. Give us the grace to return to you.
PSALM 109, NO. 2.

Ant. 2: We were ransomed with the precious blood of Christ, the lamb who is without blemish.
PSALM 110, NO. 2.

Ant. 3: Ours were the sufferings he bore, ours the sorrows he carried.
CANTICLE, I PETER 2:21-24, NO. 18.

SUNDAY 4

Ant. 1: God has appointed him to judge everyone, living and dead.
PSALM 109, NO. 2.

Ant. 2: Happy is the man to whom the Lord shows mercy; he will never waver.
PSALM 111, NO. 4.

Ant. 3: God fulfilled what he had foretold in the words of all the prophets: that Christ would suffer.
CANTICLE, 1 PETER 2:21-24, NO. 18.

Scripture Reading   *1 Corinthians 9:24-25*
All the runners at the stadium are trying to win, but only one of them gets the prize. You must run in the same way, meaning to win. All the fighters at the games go into strict training; they do this just to win a wreath that will wither away, but we do it for a wreath that will never wither.

Short Responsory
R̷ Hear us, Lord, and have mercy, for we have sinned against you.
Repeat R̷
V̷ Listen, Christ, to the prayers of those who cry to you. R̷ Glory be. R̷

Magnificat Antiphon
Sunday 1: Keep watch over us, eternal Saviour. Do not let the cunning tempter overcome us, for you have become our helper at all times.
Sunday 2: Tell no man about the vision which you have seen, until the Son of Man has risen from the dead.
Sunday 3: Whoever drinks the water that I shall give, says the Lord, will never be thirsty again.
Sunday 4: My son, you are with me always and all I have is yours. But it was right that we should celebrate and rejoice, because your brother was dead and has come to life; he was lost and is found.

Intercessions

SUNDAYS I AND 3

God the Father has chosen for himself a people, who are born again, not from any mortal seed but from his everlasting Word. Let us praise his name and turn to him in prayer.

℞ **Lord, have mercy on your people.**

Merciful God, hear our prayers for all your people;—may they hunger more for your word than for any human food. ℞

Teach us to love sincerely the people of our nation and of every race on earth;—may we work for their peace and welfare. ℞

Strengthen those who will be reborn in baptism:—make them living stones in the temple of your Spirit. ℞

May the dying go forward in hope to meet Christ, their judge;—may they see your face and be happy for ever. ℞

Our Father

SUNDAYS 2 AND 4

We give thanks to Christ, our head and our master. Let us pray to him with trust and humility, for he served all men and was good to everyone.

℞ **Lord Jesus, visit your family**

Lord, help the bishops and priests of your Church, who share in your office of head and pastor;—unite them with yourself to lead all men to the Father. ℞

Send your angels to protect those who travel;—keep them from harm and bring them safely home. ℞

Teach us to care for everyone;—make us more like you in serving others. ℞

Help us to form a human community where all men live in friendship;—Lord, unite us in your love. ℞

Show your love for the dead:—let them see the light of your face. ℞

Our Father

Concluding Prayer

Sunday 1: Through our annual Lenten observance, Lord,
deepen our understanding of the mystery of Christ,
and make it a reality in the conduct of our lives.
(We make our prayer) through our Lord.

Sunday 2: God our Father,
you bid us listen to your Son, the well-beloved.
Nourish our hearts on your word,
purify the eyes of our mind,
and fill us with joy at the vision of your glory.
(We make our prayer) through our Lord.

Sunday 3: God our Father,
in your infinite love and goodness
you have shown us that
prayer, fasting, and almsgiving
are remedies for sin:
accept the humble admission of our guilt,
and when our conscience weighs us down
let your unfailing mercy raise us up.
(We make our prayer) through our Lord.

Sunday 4: Lord God, in your surpassing wisdom
you reconcile man to yourself through your Word.
Grant that your Christian people may come with eager faith and
    ready will
to celebrate the Easter festival.
(We make our prayer) through our Lord.

SUNDAY 5 OF LENT

Hymn

Psalmody
Ant. 1: As Moses lifted up the serpent in the desert, so the Son of
Man must be lifted up.
PSALM 109, NO. 2.

Ant. 2: The Lord of hosts protects and rescues; he spares and **he**
saves.
PSALM 113A, NO. 6.
    E.P.S.—B

Ant. 3: He was wounded for our faults, he was bruised for our sins. Through his wounds we are healed.

CANTICLE, 1 PETER 2:21-24, NO. 18.

Scripture Reading   *Acts 13:26-30a*

My brothers, it is to us that this message of salvation has been sent! For the people who live in Jerusalem and their leaders did not know that he is the Saviour, nor did they understand the words of the prophets that are read every Sabbath day. Yet they made the prophets' words come true by condemning Jesus. And even though they could find no reason to pass the death sentence on him, they asked Pilate to have him put to death. And after they had done everything that the Scriptures say about him, they took him down from the cross and placed him in a grave. But God raised him from the dead.

Short Responsory

℞ Hear us, Lord, and have mercy for we have sinned against you. *Repeat* ℞

℣ Listen, Christ, to the prayers of those who cry to you. ℞ Glory be. ℞

Magnificat ant. When I am lifted up from the earth, I shall draw all men to myself.

Intercessions

God the Father has chosen for himself a people, who are born again, not from any mortal seed but from his everlasting Word. Let us praise his name and turn to him in prayer.

   ℞ **Lord, have mercy on your people.**

Merciful God, hear our prayers for all your people;—may they hunger more for your word than for any human food. ℞

Teach us to love sincerely the people of our nation and of every race on earth;—may we work for their peace and welfare. ℞

Strengthen those who will be reborn in baptism:—make them living stones in the temple of your Spirit. ℞

May the dying go forward in hope to meet Christ, their judge;— may they see your face and be happy for ever. ℞

Our Father

Concluding Prayer
Lord our God, your Son so loved the world
that he gave himself up to death for our sake.
Strengthen us by your grace,
and give us a heart willing to live by that same love.
(We make our prayer) through our Lord.

PALM SUNDAY

Hymn

Psalmody
Ant. 1: He was wounded and humbled, but God has raised him up
with his own right hand.
PSALM 109, NO. 2.

Ant. 2: The blood of Christ purifies us to serve the living God.
PSALM 113B, NO. 7.

Ant. 3: He carried our sins in his own body on the cross, so that we
might die to sin and live for holiness.
CANTICLE, I PETER 2:21-24, NO. 18.

Scripture Reading   *Acts 13:26-30a*
My brothers, it is to us that this message of salvation has been sent!
For the people who live in Jerusalem and their leaders did not
know that he is the Saviour, nor did they understand the words of
the prophets that are read every Sabbath day. Yet they made the
prophets' words come true by condemning Jesus. And even though
they could find no reason to pass the death sentence on him, they
asked Pilate to have him put to death. And after they had done
everything that the Scriptures say about him, they took him down
from the cross and placed him in a grave. But God raised him from
the dead.

Short Responsory
℟ We worship you, Christ, and we bless you. *Repeat* ℟
℣ By your cross you have redeemed the world. ℟ Glory be. ℟

Magnificat ant. It is written: "I will strike the shepherd down and the sheep of his flock will be scattered." But after my resurrection I will go before you into Galilee; there you will see me, said the Lord.

Intercessions

Let us pray humbly to the Saviour of all men. He went up to Jerusalem to endure the passion and enter into his glory.

R̠ **Sanctify the people you redeemed by your blood.**

Christ our Redeemer, let us share in your passion by works of penance;—let us attain the glory of your resurrection. R̠

Grant us the protection of your Mother, the comforter of the afflicted;—help us to extend to others the consolation you have given us. R̠

Take care of those we have discouraged and those we have wronged; —help us to learn from our sufferings so that justice and love may prevail in the end. R̠

You humbled yourself even to accepting death, death on a cross; —grant to your servants obedience and patience. R̠

Share with the dead your bodily glory;—let us rejoice one day with them in the fellowship of the saints. R̠

Our Father

Concluding Prayer

Almighty, ever-living God,
you gave our Saviour the command
to become man and undergo the cross,
as an example of humility for all men to follow.
We have the lessons of his sufferings:
give us also the fellowship of his resurrection.
(We make our prayer) through our Lord.

EASTER SUNDAY

Hymn

Psalmody
Ant. 1: Mary Magdalen came with the other Mary to see the tomb where the Lord had been laid, alleluia.
PSALM 109, NO. 2.

Ant. 2: Come and see where the Lord was laid, alleluia.
PSALM 113A, NO. 6.

Ant. 3: Jesus said, "Go, and tell my brothers that they are to leave for Galilee; they will see me there." Alleluia.
CANTICLE, REVELATION 19:1-2, 5-7, NO. 21.

Scripture Reading   *Hebrews 10:12-14*
Christ has offered one single sacrifice for sins, and then taken his place for ever at the right hand of God, where he is now waiting until his enemies are made into a footstool for him. By virtue of that one single offering he has achieved the eternal perfection of all whom he is sanctifying.

In place of the short responsory the following antiphon is said:
Ant. This is the day which was made by the Lord: let us rejoice and be glad, alleluia.

Magnificat ant. On the evening of that Sunday, when the disciples were gathered behind locked doors, Jesus came and stood among them. He said to them, "Peace be with you, alleluia."

Intercessions
Let us pray with joy to Christ the Lord. He rose from the dead and is living now to intercede for us.
℟ **Victorious king, hear us.**
Christ, you are the light of the world and the salvation of nations;
—set us on fire with your Spirit as we proclaim the wonder of your resurrection. ℟

Let Israel recognise in you the Messiah it has longed for;—fill all men with the knowledge of your glory.
℞ **Victorious king, hear us.**
Keep us united in the communion of saints;—may we find rest with them, when life's work is done. ℞
You have overcome death, the last enemy of man;—destroy everything in us that is at enmity with God. ℞
Christ, our Saviour, you became obedient to death, but God raised you to the heights;—receive our brothers into the kingdom of your glory. ℞
Our Father

Concluding Prayer
On this day, Lord God,
you opened for us the way to eternal life
through your only Son's victory over death.
Grant that as we celebrate the feast of his resurrection
we may be renewed by your Holy Spirit
and rise again in the light of life.
(We make our prayer) through our Lord.

Concluding invitation: Go in the peace of Christ, alleluia, alleluia.
℞ **Thanks be to God, alleluia, alleluia.**

Sunday 2 of Eastertide
LOW SUNDAY
The Octave Day of Easter

Hymn, antiphons, psalms and canticle as on Easter Sunday, p. 37.

Scripture Reading   *Hebrews 10:12-14*
Christ has offered one single sacrifice for sins, and then taken his place for ever at the right hand of God, where he is now waiting until his enemies are made into a footstool for him. By virtue of that one single offering he has achieved the eternal perfection of all whom he is sanctifying.

In place of the short responsory the following antiphon is said:
Ant. This is the day which was made by the Lord: let us rejoice and be glad, alleluia.

Magnificat ant. You believe because you have seen me, Thomas. Blessed are those who have never seen me and yet believe.

Intercessions

Let us pray to God the Father, who raised Jesus to life and exalted him at his own right hand.

℟ **Lord, protect your people through the glory of Christ.**

Father, through the victory of the cross you have lifted up Jesus from the earth;—may he draw all men to himself. ℟

Through the exaltation of Christ send your Spirit into the Church;
—make her the sign of unity for the whole human family. ℟

You have become the Father of men through water and the Spirit;
—keep them faithful to their baptism until they enter eternal life. ℟

Through the exaltation of your Son raise up the sorrowful, set prisoners free, heal the sick;—may the whole world rejoice in your wonderful gifts. ℟

You nourished the faithful departed with Christ's body and blood;
—let them share in his glory on the day of resurrection. ℟

Our Father

Concluding Prayer

God of eternal compassion,
each Easter you rekindle the faith of your consecrated people.
Give them still greater grace,
so that all may truly understand
the waters in which they were cleansed,
the Spirit by which they were reborn,
the blood by which they were redeemed.
(We make our prayer) through our Lord.

Concluding invitation: Go in the peace of Christ, alleluia, alleluia.
℟ **Thanks be to God, alleluia, alleluia.**

SUNDAYS 3–6 OF EASTERTIDE

Hymn

Psalmody

Ant. 1: When he had made purification for sin, he sat at the right hand of the majesty on high, alleluia.

PSALM 109, NO. 2.

Ant. 2: The Lord has delivered his people, alleluia.

PSALM 110, NO. 3.

Ant. 3: Alleluia, the Lord our God is king; let us rejoice and give glory to him, alleluia.

CANTICLE, CF REVELATION 19:1-2, 5-7, NO. 21.

SUNDAY 4

Ant. 1: You must look for the things of heaven, where Christ is, sitting at God's right hand, alleluia.

PSALM 109, NO. 2.

Ant. 2: He has risen as a light in the darkness, for the upright of heart, alleluia.

PSALM 111, NO. 4.

Ant. 3: Alleluia, victory and glory and power to our God, alleluia.

CANTICLE, CF REVELATION 19:1-2, 5-7, NO. 21.

SUNDAY 5

Ant. 1: The Lord has risen and sits at the right hand of God, alleluia.

PSALM 109, NO. 2.

Ant. 2: He has freed us from the power of darkness and has given us a place in the kingdom of his Son, alleluia.

PSALM 113A, NO. 6.

Ant. 3: Alleluia, the Lord, our God, is King; let us rejoice and give glory to him, alleluia.

CANTICLE, CF REVELATION 19:1-2, 5-7, NO. 21.

SUNDAY 6

Ant. 1: He raised Christ from the dead and placed him at his own right hand in heaven, alleluia.
PSALM 109, NO. 2.

Ant. 2: You have been converted from idolatry to the living God, alleluia.
PSALM 113B, NO. 7.

Ant. 3: Alleluia, victory and glory and power belong to our God, alleluia.
CANTICLE, CF REVELATION 19:1-2, 5-7, NO. 21.

Scripture Reading   *Hebrews 10:12-14*
Christ has offered one single sacrifice for sins, and then taken his place for ever at the right hand of God, where he is now waiting until his enemies are made into a footstool for him. By virtue of that one single offering he has achieved the eternal perfection of all whom he is sanctifying.

Short Responsory
R̸ The Lord has truly risen, alleluia, alleluia. *Repeat* R̸
V̸ He has appeared to Simon. R̸ Glory be. R̸

Magnificat Antiphon
Sunday 3: Jesus said to his disciples, "Bring some of the fish you have just caught." Simon Peter went aboard and dragged the net to the shore, full of fish, alleluia.
Sunday 4: The sheep that belong to me listen to my voice; and I, the Lord, know them, alleluia.
Sunday 5: I give you a new commandment: love one another, as I have loved you, says the Lord, alleluia.
Sunday 6: If anyone loves me he will keep my word, and my Father will love him, and we shall come to him and make our home with him, alleluia.

Intercessions
SUNDAYS 3 AND 5
Let us pray with joy to Christ the Lord. He rose from the dead and

is living now to intercede for us.

℟ **Victorious king, hear us.**

Christ, you are the light of the world and the salvation of nations;
—set us on fire with your Spirit as we proclaim the wonder of your
resurrection. ℟

Let Israel recognise in you the Messiah they have longed for:—
fill all men with the knowledge of your glory. ℟

Keep us united in the communion of saints;—may we find rest
with them, when life's work is done. ℟

You have overcome death, the last enemy of man;—destroy everything in us that is at enmity with God. ℟

Christ, our Saviour, you became obedient to death, but God raised
you to the heights:—receive our brothers into the kingdom of your
glory. ℟

Our Father

SUNDAYS 4 AND 6

Let us pray to God the Father, who raised Jesus to life and exalted
him at his own right hand.

℟ **Lord, protect your people through the glory of Christ.**

Father, through the victory of the cross you have lifted up Jesus
from the earth;—may he draw all men to himself. ℟

Through the exaltation of Christ send your Spirit into the Church;
—make her the sign of unity for the whole human family. ℟

You have become the Father of men through water and the Spirit;
—keep them faithful to their baptism until they enter eternal life. ℟

Through the exaltation of your Son raise up the sorrowful, set
prisoners free, heal the sick;—may the whole world rejoice in your
wonderful gifts. ℟

You nourished the faithful departed with Christ's body and blood;
—let them share in his glory on the day of resurrection. ℟

Our Father

Concluding Prayer
Sunday 3: Lord God,
grant your people constant joy
in the renewed vigour of their souls.
They rejoice because you have restored them

to the glory of your adopted children:
let them look forward gladly
in the certain hope of resurrection.
(We make our prayer) through our Lord.

Sunday 4: Almighty, ever-living God,
bring us to the joy of your heavenly city:
so that we, your little flock,
may follow where Christ, our Good Shepherd,
has gone before us by the power of his resurrection.
(We make our prayer) through our Lord.

Sunday 5: Since it is from you, God our Father,
that redemption comes to us, your adopted children:
look with favour on the family you love,
give true freedom to us and to all who believe in Christ,
and bring us all alike to our eternal heritage.
(We make our prayer) through our Lord.

Sunday 6: Almighty God,
give us the grace of an attentive love
to celebrate these days of joy
devoted to the honour of the Risen Lord.
Teach us to hold fast in our actions
to the mystery we recall in worship.
(We make our prayer) through our Lord.

THE ASCENSION OF THE LORD
Solemnity

Hymn

Psalmody
Ant. 1: He ascended to heaven and is seated at the right hand of the
Father, alleluia.
PSALM 109, NO. 2.

Ant. 2: God goes up with shouts of joy; the Lord ascends with trumpet blast, alleluia.

PSALM 46, NO. I.

Ant. 3: Now the Son of Man has been glorified, and in him God has been glorified, alleluia.

CANTICLE, REVELATION II:17-18; 12:10b-12a, NO. 19.

Scripture Reading   *1 Peter 3:18, 22*

Christ himself, innocent though he was, died once for sins, died for the guilty, to lead us to God. In the body, he was put to death, in the spirit he was raised to life. He has entered heaven and is at God's right hand, now that he has made the angels and Dominations and Powers his subjects.

Short Responsory

℟ I am ascending to my Father and your Father, alleluia, alleluia. *Repeat* ℟

℣ I go to my God and your God. ℟ Glory be. ℟

Magnificat ant. King of Glory, Lord Almighty, today you have ascended victoriously above the heavens: do not leave us as orphans without a guide, but send the one whom you promised, the gift of the Father, the Spirit of Truth, alleluia.

Intercessions

Let us pray to the Lord who is now lifted up from the earth, drawing all things to himself.

℟ **You, Christ, are the king of glory.**

Lord Jesus, you offered one sacrifice for sin and then ascended in victory to the Father;—achieve the eternal perfection of those whom you are sanctifying. ℟

Eternal priest, minister of the new covenant, you are alive and interceding for us;—save your people who turn to you in prayer. ℟

After your passion, you appeared to your disciples, and they knew you to be alive:—strengthen our belief that you are with us today. ℟

On this day you promised the Holy Spirit to the apostles, for the

spreading of your gospel to the ends of the earth;—strengthen us by the power of the Spirit in bearing witness before the world. ℟
Our Father

Concluding Prayer
Almighty God,
fill us with a holy joy,
teach us how to thank you with reverence and love
on account of the ascension of Christ your Son.
You have raised us up with him:
where he, the head, has preceded us in glory,
there we, the body, are called in hope.
(We make our prayer) through our Lord.

SUNDAY 7 OF EASTERTIDE

Hymn

Psalmody
Ant. 1: When he had made purification for sin, he sat at the right hand of the Majesty on high, alleluia.
PSALM 109, NO. 2.

Ant. 2: The Lord has delivered his people, alleluia.
PSALM 110, NO. 3.

Ant. 3: Alleluia, the Lord our God is king; let us rejoice and give glory to him, alleluia.
CANTICLE, CF REVELATION 19:1-2, 5-7, NO. 21.

Scripture Reading   *Hebrews 10:12-14*
Christ has offered one single sacrifice for sins, and then taken his place for ever at the right hand of God, where he is now waiting until his enemies are made into a footstool for him. By virtue of that one single offering he has achieved the eternal perfection of all whom he is sanctifying.

Short Responsory

℟ The Holy Spirit is the Advocate, alleluia, alleluia. *Repeat* ℟
℣ He will teach you everything. ℟ Glory be. ℟

Magnificat ant. I will send you the Advocate, the Spirit of truth who comes from the Father. He will be my witness, alleluia.

Intercessions

Christ our Lord urged us to pray and the Holy Spirit came to fill our hearts and minds.

   ℟ **May the Holy Spirit plead for us.**

Eternal shepherd, give to the pastors of your Church wisdom and understanding;—may they lead your faithful people in the way of salvation. ℟

Heavenly Christ, you are rich in mercy and compassion;—do not forget the poor and the needy you have left behind on earth. ℟

By the power of the Holy Spirit you were conceived of the Virgin Mary;—preserve in religious women the spirit of loving service. ℟

Christ, our priest, you give glory to the Father in the Holy Spirit;—unite all men together in your hymn of praise. ℟

Grant to the dead the glorious freedom of God's sons—and the completion of bodily redemption. ℟

Our Father

Concluding Prayer

Lord God,
we believe that the Saviour of mankind
is enthroned with you in majesty.
Listen to our prayer,
and, according to his promise,
let us feel his presence among us
until the end of time.
(We make our prayer) through our Lord.

PENTECOST SUNDAY

Hymn

Psalmody
Ant. 1: The Spirit of the Lord has filled the whole world, alleluia.
PSALM 109, NO. 2.

Ant. 2: Send forth your power, Lord, from your holy temple in Jerusalem, and bring to perfection your work among us, alleluia.
PSALM 113A, NO. 6.

Ant. 3: They were all filled with the Holy Spirit and began to speak, alleluia.
CANTICLE, REVELATION 19:1-2, 5-7, NO. 21.

Scripture Reading   *Ephesians 4:3-6*
Do your best to preserve the unity which the Spirit gives, by the peace that binds you together. There is one Body and one Spirit, just as there is one hope to which God has called you. There is one Lord, one faith, one baptism; there is one God and Father of all men, who is Lord of all, works through all, and is in all.

Short Responsory
℞ The Spirit of the Lord has filled the whole world, alleluia, alleluia. *Repeat* ℞
℣ It is he who holds all things in being and understands every word that is spoken. ℞ Glory be. ℞

Magnificat ant. This is the day of Pentecost, alleluia; today the Holy Spirit appeared to the disciples in the form of fire and gave to them his special gifts; he sent them into the world to proclaim that whoever believes and is baptised will be saved, alleluia.

Intercessions
We know that the Father is with us because of the Spirit he has given us. With this confidence we turn to you in prayer:
   ℞ **Father, send your Spirit into the Church!**

Father, you want to unite all men by baptism in the Spirit;—draw all believers together in mind and heart.

R̷ Father, send your Spirit into the Church!

You sent the Spirit to fill the earth with your love;—let men build the human city in justice and peace. R̷

Lord God, Father of all men, bring to your scattered children unity of faith:—make the world alive with the power of your Spirit. R̷

By the work of the Spirit you create all minds afresh:—heal the sick, comfort the afflicted, and bring all men to salvation. R̷

Through the Holy Spirit you raised your Son from the dead.—Raise us by the power of your Spirit when we come to your kingdom. R̷

Our Father

Concluding Prayer

Lord God,
you sanctify your Church in every race and nation
by the mystery we celebrate on this day.
Pour out the gifts of the Holy Spirit on all mankind,
and fulfil now in the hearts of your faithful
what you accomplished
when the Gospel was first preached on earth.
(We make our prayer) through our Lord.

The invitation to leave is:

Go in the peace of Christ, alleluia, alleluia.

R̷ Thanks be to God, alleluia, alleluia.

Sunday after Pentecost
THE MOST HOLY TRINITY
Solemnity

Hymn

Psalmody

Ant. 1: O true, highest and everlasting Trinity, Father, Son and

Holy Spirit.
PSALM 109, NO. 2.

Ant. 2: Give us freedom, salvation and life, O blessed Trinity.
PSALM 113A, NO. 6.

Ant. 3: Holy, holy, holy is the Lord God almighty, who was, who is, and who is to come.
CANTICLE, CF REVELATION 19:1-2, 5-7, NO. 21.

Scripture Reading   *Ephesians 4:3-6*
Do your best to preserve the unity which the Spirit gives, by the peace that binds you together. There is one body and one Spirit, just as there is one hope to which God has called you. There is one Lord, one faith, one baptism; there is one God and Father of all men, who is Lord of all, works through all and is in all.

Short Responsory
R̶ Let us bless the Father and the Son with the Holy Spirit. Let us praise him for ever. *Repeat* R̶
V̶ To God alone be all honour and glory. R̶ Glory be. R̶

Magnificat ant. With our heart and lips we praise you, we worship you and we bless you, God the Father unbegotten, only-begotten Son, and Holy Spirit Paraclete: all glory is yours for ever.

Intercessions
Father, through your Holy Spirit you gave Christ your Son to us in the flesh, so that we might have life through him. Filled now with that life, we raise our hearts in praise of the Holy Trinity, saying:
> R̶ **Glory be to the Father and to the Son and to the Holy Spirit.**
Father almighty, eternal God, in the name of your Son send your Holy Spirit upon the Church:—may the Comforter preserve us in unity, harmony and the fulness of truth. R̶
Lord, send your labourers into the harvest to teach all nations and baptise them in the name of the Father and of the Son and of the Holy Spirit:—strengthen them all in the faith. R̶
Lord, support all those who suffer persecution on account of their

faith in your Son:—give them the Spirit of truth who will, according to his promise, speak through them.

℟ **Glory be to the Father and to the Son and to the Holy Spirit.**

Father almighty, all acknowledge that you, the Word and the Spirit are one:—as we believe in one God, so may we hope in you and love you. ℟

Father of the living, bring those who have died to share your glory: —with your Son and the Holy Spirit may they reign eternally with you in heaven. ℟

Our Father

Concluding Prayer
God our Father,
you revealed the great mystery of your godhead to men
when you sent into the world
the Word who is Truth
and the Spirit who makes us holy.
Help us to believe in you and worship you,
as the true faith teaches:
three Persons, eternal in glory,
one God, infinite in majesty.
(We make our prayer) through our Lord.

Thursday after Holy Trinity

THE BODY AND BLOOD OF CHRIST
Corpus Christi   Solemnity

Hymn

Psalmody
Ant. 1: Christ the Lord is a priest for ever. Like Melchizedek, he made an offering of bread and wine.
PSALM 109, NO. 2.

Ant. 2: I will take the chalice of salvation and I will offer a thanksgiving sacrifice.
PSALM 115, NO. 8.

Ant. 3: You are the Way, you are the Truth, you, O Lord, are the Life of the world.

CANTICLE, CF REVELATION 19:1-2, 5-7, NO. 21.

Scripture Reading *1 Corinthians 11:23-25*

This is what I received from the Lord, and in turn passed on to you: that on the same night that he was betrayed, the Lord Jesus took some bread, and thanked God for it and broke it, and he said: "This is my body which is for you; do this as a memorial of me." In the same way he took the cup after supper, and said: "This cup is the new covenant in my blood. Whenever you drink it, do this as a memorial of me."

Short Responsory

R̞ He gave them the bread of heaven to eat, alleluia, alleluia. *Repeat* R̞
℣ Man has tasted the food of angels. R̞ Glory be. R̞

Magnificat ant. O sacred feast in which we partake of Christ: his sufferings are remembered, our minds are filled with his grace and we receive a pledge of the glory that is to be ours, alleluia.

Intercessions

At the supper to which all are invited, Christ gives his body and blood for the life of the world. Earnestly we beseech him, saying:
  R̞ **Lord Jesus Christ, give us the bread of eternal life.**
Lord Jesus Christ, Son of the living God, you have commanded us to celebrate the eucharistic meal in remembrance of you:— enrich your Church with the worthy celebration of these mysteries. R̞
Lord Jesus Christ, eternal high priest, you have committed to your priests the ministration of your sacraments:—help them to do their part in your work with the unfailing gladness of genuine charity. R̞
Lord Jesus Christ, manna from heaven, you make into one all who share the one bread:—grant peace and concord to all who believe in you. R̞

Lord Jesus Christ, heavenly physician, you give an eternal remedy and a pledge of resurrection to those who eat your bread:—grant health to the ailing and a real hope to sinners.

℟ **Lord Jesus Christ, give us the bread of eternal life.**

Lord Jesus Christ, king who is to come, we know that whenever we celebrate these mysteries, we proclaim your death until you come again:—bring all those who have died in you to share your resurrection. ℟

Our Father

Concluding Prayer
Lord Jesus Christ,
you gave your Church an admirable sacrament
as the abiding memorial of your passion.
Teach us so to worship
the sacred mystery of your Body and Blood,
that its redeeming power
may sanctify us always.
Who live and reign with the Father and the Holy Spirit,
God, for ever and ever.

Friday after the Second Sunday after Pentecost
THE MOST SACRED HEART OF JESUS
Solemnity

Hymn

Psalmody
Ant. 1: With your gentle yoke, Lord, rule in the midst of your foes.
PSALM 109, NO. 2.

Ant. 2: The Lord is compassion and love: he gives food to those who fear him.
PSALM 110, NO. 3.

Ant. 3: This is the Lamb of God, this is he who takes away the sins of the world.
CANTICLE, PHILIPPIANS 2:6-11, NO. 16.

Scripture Reading   *Ephesians 2:4-7*
God's mercy is so abundant, and his love for us is so great, that while we were spiritually dead in our disobedience, he brought us to life with Christ; it is by God's grace that you have been saved. In our union with Christ Jesus, he raised us up with him to rule with him in the heavenly world. He did this to demonstrate for all time to come the abundant riches of his grace in the love he showed us in Christ Jesus.

Short Responsory
R̂ Christ loved us and washed away our sins with his blood. *Repeat* R̂
V̂ He made us a kingdom and priests to serve his God and Father. R̂ Glory be. R̂

Magnificat ant. The Lord has received us into his own self, into his heart, remembering his mercy, alleluia.

Intercessions
We make our prayers to Jesus, in whom we find rest for our souls. and we say to him: R̂ **Beloved Lord, have mercy on us.**
Jesus, your heart was pierced by the lance and from it flowed blood and water so that your bride, the Church, might be born:— keep her in holiness without spot or wrinkle. R̂
Jesus, holy temple of God, you were condemned by men and raised up by the Father:—make the Church the tabernacle of the Most High. R̂
Jesus, king and centre of all hearts, in your loving mercy you never cease to draw us to yourself:—keep alive your covenant with us all. R̂
Jesus, our peace and reconciliation, from the cross you forgave your enemies and you bring all men together in peace:—show us how to reach the Father. R̂
Jesus, our life and resurrection, you lighten our burden and give rest to our souls:—draw all sinners to yourself. R̂
Jesus, because of your infinite love you were obedient even unto death on a cross:—bring to life all those who are sleeping in peace. R̂
Our Father

Concluding Prayer
Almighty God, and Father
we glory in the Sacred Heart of Jesus, your beloved Son,
as we call to mind the great things his love has done for us.
Fill us with the grace that flows in abundance
from the Heart of Jesus, the source of heaven's gifts.
(We make our prayer) through our Lord.

Last Sunday of the Year
CHRIST THE KING

Hymn

Psalmody
Ant. 1: He will sit on the throne of David and will rule his kingdom
for ever, alleluia.
PSALM 109, NO. 2.

Ant. 2: Yours is an everlasting kingdom; Lord, your rule lasts from
age to age.
PSALM 144, NO. 13.

Ant. 3: On his cloak and on his thigh there was a name written:
The King of kings and the Lord of lords. To him be glory and
honour for ever and ever.
CANTICLE, CF REVELATION 19:1-2, 5-7, NO. 21.

Scripture Reading   *1 Corinthians 15:25-28*
He must be king until he has put all his enemies under his feet, and
the last of the enemies to be destroyed is death, for everything is to
be put under his feet. Though when it is said that everything is
subjected, this clearly cannot include the One who subjected everything to him. And when everything is subjected to him, then the
Son himself will be subject in his turn to the One who subjected all
things to him, so that God may be all in all.

Short Responsory

℞ Your throne, O God, shall stand for ever and ever. *Repeat* ℞
℣ The sceptre of your kingdom is a sceptre of justice. ℞ Glory be. ℞

Magnificat ant. All authority in heaven and on earth has been given to me, says the Lord.

Intercessions

To Christ our King, who is first in all things and in whom all things exist, let us confidently pray: ℞ **Lord, may your kingdom come.**

Lord Jesus Christ, our king and our shepherd, gather your flock from every corner of the earth:—protect it in your fresh and fertile pastures. ℞

Jesus, our leader and Saviour, make all people your own; heal the sick, seek out the lost, preserve the strong:—bring back the strayed, reunite those who are scattered and give new hope to the down-hearted. ℞

Jesus, eternal judge, when you hand over your kingdom to your Father, remember us, your faithful people:—let us take possession of the kingdom prepared for us since the foundation of the world. ℞

Jesus, prince of peace, remove from men's hearts the greed that leads to war:—speak words of peace to your people. ℞

Jesus, heir of all nations, bring all mankind to the kingdom of your Church, entrusted to you by the Father:—move all men to acknowledge you as the Head in the unity of the Holy Spirit. ℞

Jesus, first-born of all creation and first to be born from the dead:—bring all the departed to the glory of your resurrection. ℞

Our Father

Concluding Prayer

Almighty, ever-living God,
it is your will
to unite the entire universe
under your beloved Son,
Jesus Christ, the King of heaven and earth.
Grant freedom to the whole of creation,
and let it praise and serve your majesty for ever.
(We make our prayer) through our Lord.

THROUGH THE YEAR

SUNDAY: WEEK 1

℣ O God, come to our aid.
℟ **O Lord, make haste to help us.**
Glory be to the Father . . .

Hymn

Psalmody
Ant. 1: The Lord will send his mighty sceptre from Sion, and he will rule for ever, alleluia.

THE MESSIAH IS KING AND PRIEST   PSALM 109(110):1-5, 7
He must be king so that he may put all his enemies under his feet
(1 Corinthians 15:25)

The Lórd's revelátion to my Máster:†
"Sít on my ríght:*
your fóes I will pút beneath your féet."

The Lórd will wíeld from Síon†
your scéptre of pówer:*
rúle in the mídst of all your fóes.

A prínce from the dáy of your bírth†
on the hóly móuntains;*
from the wómb before the dáwn I begót you.

The Lórd has sworn an óath he will not chánge.†
"You are a príest for éver,*
a príest like Melchízedek of óld."

The Máster stánding at your ríght hand*
will shatter kíngs in the dáy of his wráth.

He shall drínk from the stréam by the wáyside*
and thérefore he shall líft up his héad.

Glory be to the Father . . .

Ant. The Lord will send his mighty sceptre from Sion, and he will rule for ever, alleluia.
Ant. 2: The earth trembled before the Lord, alleluia.

ISRAEL IS FREED FROM EGYPT   PSALM 113A(114):1-8
You, who have renounced this world, have also been led forth from Egypt (St Augustine)

When Ísrael came fórth from Égypt,*
Jacob's sóns from an álien péople,
Júdah becáme the Lord's témple,*
Ísrael becáme his kíngdom.

The séa fléd at the síght:*
the Jórdan turned báck on it cóurse,
the móuntains léapt like ráms*
and the hílls like yéarling shéep.

Whý was it, séa, that you fléd,*
that you túrned back, Jórdan, on your cóurse?
Móuntains, that you léapt like ráms,*
hílls, like yéarling shéep?

Trémble, O éarth, before the Lórd,*
in the présence of the Gód of Jácob,
who túrns the róck into a poól*
and flínt into a spríng of wáter.

Glory be to the Father . . .

Ant. The earth trembled before the Lord, alleluia.
Ant. 3: The Lord is King, our God, the Almighty! alleluia.

When chanted, the following canticle is sung with Alleluia *as set out. When recited, it suffices to say* Alleluia *at the beginning and end of each strophe.*

THE MARRIAGE FEAST OF THE LAMB   CANTICLE
                                                    CF REVELATION 19:1-2, 5-7

Alleluia.
Salvation and glory and power belong to our God,*
(R⁄ Alleluia)
His judgements are true and just.
R⁄ Alleluia (alleluia).

Alleluia.
Praise our God, all you his servants,*
(R⁄ Alleluia).
You who fear him, small and great.
R⁄ Alleluia (alleluia).

Alleluia.
The Lord our God, the Almighty, reigns,*
(R⁄ Alleluia.)
Let us rejoice and exult and give him the glory.
R⁄ Alleluia (alleluia).

Alleluia.
The marriage of the Lamb has come,*
(R⁄ Alleluia.)
And his bride has made herself ready.
R⁄ Alleluia (alleluia).

Glory be to the Father . . .

Ant. The Lord is King, our God, the Almighty! alleluia.

Scripture Reading   *2 Corinthians 1:3-4*
Let us give thanks to the God and Father of our Lord Jesus Christ,
the merciful Father, the God from whom all help comes! He helps
us in all our troubles, so that we are able to help those who have all
kinds of troubles, using the same help that we ourselves have received from God.

Short Responsory
Cantor: Blessed are you in the vault of heaven.
All: **Blessed are you in the vault of heaven.**

Cantor: You are exalted and glorified above all else for ever.
All: **Blessed are you in the vault of heaven.**
Cantor: Glory be to the Father and to the Son and to the Holy
Spirit.
All: **Blessed are you in the vault of heaven.**

Magnificat
The antiphon varies each week. See pp. 74ff.

My soul glorifies the Lord,*
my spirit rejoices in God, my Saviour.
He looks on his servant in her lowliness;*
henceforth all ages will call me blessed.

The Almighty works marvels for me.*
Holy his name!
His mercy is from age to age,*
on those who fear him.

He puts forth his arm in strength*
and scatters the proud-hearted.
He casts the mighty from their thrones*
and raises the lowly.

He fills the starving with good things,*
sends the rich away empty.

He protects Israel, his servant,*
remembering his mercy,
the mercy promised to our fathers,*
to Abraham and his sons for ever.

Glory be to the Father . . .

Repeat Magnificat antiphon.

Intercessions
Christ is the Head of his body, the Church, and we are the members of that body; gathered this evening to pray in his name, we
say: ℟ **Your kingdom come!**
May your Church be a light to the nations, the sign and source of

your power to unite all men:—may she lead mankind to the mystery of your love. ℟ **Your kingdom come.**

Guide the Pope and all the bishops of your Church:—grant them the gifts of unity, of love, and of peace. ℟

Lord, give peace to our troubled world;—and give to your children security of mind and freedom from anxiety. ℟

Help us to bring your compassion to the poor, the sick, the lonely, the unloved:—lead us to find you in the coming week. ℟

Awaken the dead to a glorious resurrection:—may we be united with them at the end of time. ℟

Our Father

Concluding Prayer varies each week. See pp. 74ff.
Conclusion, as on p. 13.

SUNDAY: WEEK 2

℣ O God, come to our aid.
℟ **O Lord, make haste to help us.**
Glory be to the Father . . .

Hymn

Psalmody
Ant. 1: Christ the Lord is a priest for ever according to the order of Melchizedek, alleluia.

THE MESSIAH IS KING AND PRIEST   PSALM 109(110):1-5, 7
He must be king so that he will put all his enemies under his feet
(1 Corinthians 15:25)

The Lórd's revelátion to my Máster:†
"Sít on my ríght:*
your fóes I will pút beneath your féet."

The Lórd will wíeld from Síon†
your scéptre of pówer:*
rúle in the mídst of all your fóes.

A prínce from the dáy of your bírth†
on the hóly móuntains;*
from the wómb before the dáwn I begót you.

The Lórd has sworn an óath he will not chánge.†
"You are a príest for éver,*
a príest like Melchízedek of óld."

The Máster stánding at your ríght hand*
will shatter kíngs in the dáy of his wráth.

He shall drínk from the stréam by the wáyside*
and thérefore he shall líft up his héad.

Glory be to the Father . . .

Ant. Christ the Lord is a priest for ever according to the order of
Melchizedek, alleluia.
Ant. 2: Our God is in heaven: he has power to do whatever he will,
alleluia.

PRAISE OF THE GOD OF TRUTH   PSALM 113B(115)
Turn away from idols and worship the living and true God (1 Thessalonians 1:9)

Not to ús, Lórd, not to ús,*
but to yóur náme give the glóry
for the sáke of your lóve and your trúth,*
lest the héathen say: "Whére is their Gód?"

But our Gód is ín the héavens;*
he dóes whatéver he wílls.
Their ídols are sílver and góld,*
the wórk of húman hánds.

They have móuths but they cánnot spéak;*
they have éyes but they cánnot sée;
they have éars but they cánnot héar;*
they have nóstrils but they cánnot sméll.

With their hánds they cánnot féel;†
with their féet they cánnot wálk.*

No sóund cómes from their thróats.
Their mákers will cóme to be líke them*
and so will áll who trúst in thém.

Sons of Ísrael, trúst in the Lórd;*
hé is their hélp and their shíeld.
Sons of Áaron, trúst in the Lórd;*
hé is their hélp and their shíeld.

You who féar him, trúst in the Lórd;*
hé is their hélp and their shíeld.
He remémbers us, and hé will bléss us;†
he will bléss the sóns of Ísrael.*
He will bléss the sóns of Áaron.

The Lord will bléss thóse who féar him,*
the líttle no léss than the gréat:
to yoú may the Lórd grant íncrease,*
to yóu and áll your chíldren.

May yóu be bléssed by the Lórd,*
the máker of héaven and éarth.
The héavens belóng to the Lórd*
but the éarth he has gíven to mén.

The déad shall not práise the Lórd,*
nor thóse who go dówn into the sílence.
But wé who líve bless the Lórd*
nów and for éver. Amén.

Glory be to the Father . . .

Ant. Our God is in heaven; he has power to do whatever he will, alleluia.
Ant. 3: Praise God, all you his servants, both great and small, alleluia.

When chanted, the following canticle is sung with Alleluia *as set out. When recited, it suffices to say* Alleluia *at the beginning and end of each strophe.*

THE MARRIAGE FEAST OF THE LAMB   CANTICLE
                                        CF REVELATION 19:1-2, 5-7

Alleluia.
Salvation and glory and power belong to our God,*
(R̹ Alleluia.)
His judgements are true and just.
R̹ Alleluia (alleluia).

Alleluia.
Praise our God, all you his servants,*
(R̹ Alleluia.)
You who fear him, small and great.
R̹ Alleluia (alleluia).

Alleluia.
The Lord our God, the Almighty, reigns,*
(R̹ Alleluia.)
Let us rejoice and exult and give him the glory.
R̹ Alleluia (alleluia).

Alleluia.
The marriage of the Lamb has come,*
(R̹ Alleluia.)
And his bride has made herself ready.
R̹ Alleluia (alleluia).

Glory be to the Father . . .

Ant. Praise God, all you his servants, both great and small, alleluia.

Scripture Reading   *2 Thessalonians 2:13-14*
We feel that we must be continually thanking God for you, brothers
whom the Lord loves, because God chose you as first fruits to be
saved by the sanctifying Spirit and by faith in the truth. Through
the Good News that we brought he called you to this so that you
should share the glory of our Lord Jesus Christ.

Short Responsory
Cantor: Great is our Lord; great is his might.
All: **Great is our Lord; great is his might.**

Cantor: His wisdom can never be measured.
All: **Great is our Lord; great is his might.**
Cantor: Glory be to the Father and to the Son and to the Holy Spirit.
All: **Great is our Lord; great is his might.**

Magnificat
The antiphon varies each week. See pp. 74ff.

My soul glorifies the Lord,*
my spirit rejoices in God, my Saviour.
He looks on his servant in her lowliness;*
henceforth all ages will call me blessed.

The Almighty works marvels for me.*
Holy his name!
His mercy is from age to age,*
on those who fear him.

He puts forth his arm in strength*
and scatters the proud-hearted.
He casts the mighty from their thrones*
and raises the lowly.

He fills the starving with good things,*
sends the rich away empty.

He protects Israel, his servant,*
remembering his mercy,
the mercy promised to our fathers,*
to Abraham and his sons for ever.

Glory be to the Father . . .

Repeat Magnificat antiphon.

Intercessions
Through the gospel, the Lord Jesus calls us to share in his glory.
Let us make our prayer with him to our heavenly Father.
℟ **Lord, in your mercy hear our prayer.**

We pray for all nations:—that they may seek the way that leads to
peace, that human rights and freedom may be everywhere re-
spected, and that the world's resources may be generously shared.
℞
We pray for the Church:—that her leaders may be faithful ministers
of your word, that all her members may be strong in faith and hope
and that you may be recognised in the love she bears to all. ℞
We pray for our families, and the community in which we live:—
that we may find you in them. ℞
We pray for ourselves:—that in the coming week we may serve
others in our work, and find peace when we rest. ℞
We pray for the faithful departed:— that through your mercy they
may rest in peace. ℞
Our Father

Concluding Prayer varies each week. See pp. 74ff.
Conclusion, as on p. 13.

SUNDAY: WEEK 3

℣ O God, come to our aid.
℞ **O Lord, make haste to help us.**
Glory be to the Father . . .

Hymn

Psalmody
Ant. 1: The Lord's revelation to my Master: "Sit on my right,"
alleluia.†

THE MESSIAH IS KING AND PRIEST   PSALM 109(110):1-5, 7
He must be king so that he may put all his enemies under his feet
(1 Corinthians 15:25)

The Lórd's revelátion to my Máster:†
"Sít on my ríght:*
your fóes I will pút beneath your féet."
  E.P.S.—C

The Lórd will wíeld from Síon†
your scéptre of pówer:*
Rúle in the mídst of all your fóes.

A prínce from the dáy of your bírth†
on the hóly móuntains;*
from the wómb before the dáwn I begót you.

The Lórd has sworn an óath he will not chánge.†
"You are a príest for éver,*
a príest like Melchízedek of óld."

The Máster stánding at your ríght hand*
will shatter kíngs in the dáy of his wráth.

He shall drínk from the stréam by the wáyside*
and thérefore he shall líft up his héad.

Glory be to the Father . . .

Ant. The Lord's revelation to my Master: "Sit on my right,"
alleluia.
Ant. 2: The Lord is full of merciful love; he makes us remember
his wonders, alleluia.

GREAT ARE THE WORKS OF THE LORD   PSALM 110(111)
How great and wonderful are all your works, Lord God Almighty
(Revelation 15:3)

I will thánk the Lórd with all my héart*
in the méeting of the júst and their assémbly.
Gréat are the wórks of the Lórd;*
to be póndered by áll who lóve them.

Majéstic and glórious his wórk,*
his jústice stands fírm for éver.
He mákes us remémber his wónders.*
The Lórd is compássion and lóve.

He gives fóod to thóse who féar him;*
keeps his cóvenant éver in mínd.

He has shówn his míght to his péople*
by gíving them the lánds of the nátions.

His wórks are jústice and trúth:*
his précepts are áll of them súre,
standing fírm for éver and éver:*
they are máde in úprightness and trúth.

He has sént delíverance to his péople†
and estáblished his cóvenant for éver.*
Hóly his náme, to be féared.

To fear the Lórd is the first stage of wísdom;
all who dó so próve themselves wíse.*
His práise shall lást for éver!

Glory be to the Father . . .

Ant. The Lord is full of merciful love; he makes us remember his
wonders, alleluia.
Ant. 3: The Lord our God almighty is king, alleluia.

When chanted, the following canticle is sung with Alleluia *as set out.*
When recited, it suffices to say Alleluia *at the beginning and end of*
each strophe.

THE MARRIAGE FEAST OF THE LAMB   CANTICLE
                                    CF REVELATION 19:1-2, 5-7

Alleluia.
Salvation and glory and power belong to our God,*
(℞ Alleluia.)
His judgements are true and just.
℞ Alleluia (alleluia).

Alleluia.
Praise our God, all you his servants,*
(℞ Alleluia.)
You who fear him, small and great.
℞ Alleluia (alleluia).

Alleluia.
The Lord our God, the Almighty, reigns,*
(℞ Alleluia.)
Let us rejoice and exult and give him the glory.
℞ Alleluia (alleluia).

Alleluia.
The marriage of the Lamb has come,*
(℞ Alleluia.)
And his bride has made herself ready.
℞ Alleluia (alleluia).

Glory be to the Father . . .

Ant. The Lord our God almighty is king, alleluia.

Scripture Reading   *1 Peter 1:3-5*
Blessed be God the Father of our Lord Jesus Christ, who in his
great mercy has given us a new birth as his sons, by raising Jesus
Christ from the dead, so that we have a sure hope and the promise
of an inheritance that can never be spoilt or soiled and never fade
away, because it is being kept for you in the heavens. Through your
faith, God's power will guard you until the salvation which has
been prepared is revealed at the end of time.

Short Responsory
Cantor: Blessed are you, O Lord, in the vault of heaven.
All: **Blessed are you, O Lord, in the vault of heaven.**
Cantor: You are exalted and glorified above all else for ever.
All: **Blessed are you, O Lord, in the vault of heaven.**
Cantor: Glory be to the Father, and to the Son, and to the Holy
          Spirit.
All: **Blessed are you, O Lord, in the vault of heaven.**

Magnificat
The Antiphon varies each week. See pp. 74ff.

My soul glorifies the Lord,*
my spirit rejoices in God, my Saviour.
He looks on his servant in her lowliness;*
henceforth all ages will call me blessed.

The Almighty works marvels for me.*
Holy his name!
His mercy is from age to age,*
on those who fear him.

He puts forth his arm in strength*
and scatters the proud-hearted.
He casts the mighty from their thrones*
and raises the lowly.

He fills the starving with good things,*
sends the rich away empty.

He protects Israel, his servant,*
remembering his mercy,
the mercy promised to our fathers,*
to Abraham and his sons for ever.

Glory be to the Father . . .

Repeat Magnificat antiphon.

Intercessions
God is ever creative. His love renews all things and is the source of
our hope. Let us turn to him in confidence:
℟ **Lord, accept our thanks and our prayers.**
We give thanks for the order of created things:—you have blessed
us with the resources of the earth and the gift of human life. ℟
We give thanks for man's share in your continuing work of creation:
—we praise you for your gifts to him of inventive skill and creative
vision. ℟
We pray for all the nations of the world:—may those in authority
work for peace and goodwill among men. ℟
We pray for all who are homeless today:—we pray for families
searching for a place to live, and for refugees driven from their
homeland. ℟
Life was your first gift to us:—may those who have died come to
its fulness in you. ℟
Our Father

Concluding Prayer varies each week. See pp.74ff. Conclusion, as on p.13.

℣ O God, come to our aid.
℟ **O Lord, make haste to help us.**
Glory be to the Father . . .

Hymn

Psalmody
Ant. 1: In holy splendour I begot you before the dawn, alleluia.

THE MESSIAH IS KING AND PRIEST   PSALM 109(110):1-5, 7
He must be king so that he will put all his enemies under his feet
(1 Corinthians 15:25)

The Lórd's revelátion to my Máster:†
"Sít on my ríght:*
your fóes I will pút beneath your féet."

The Lórd will wíeld from Síon†
your scéptre of pówer:*
rúle in the mídst of all your fóes.

A prínce from the dáy of your bírth†
on the hóly móuntains;*
from the wómb before the dáwn I begót you.

The Lórd has sworn an óath he will not chánge.†
"You are a príest for éver,*
a príest like Melchízedek of óld."

The Máster stánding at your ríght hand*
will shatter kíngs in the dáy of his wráth.

He shall drínk from the stréam by the wáyside*
and thérefore he shall líft up his héad.

Glory be to the Father . . .

Ant. In holy splendour I begot you before the dawn, alleluia.

Ant. 2: Blessed are those who hunger and thirst for justice, for they shall have their fill.

THE HAPPINESS OF A JUST MAN   PSALM III(112)
Be like children of the light; for the fruits of the light are seen in complete goodness and right living and truth (Ephesians 5:8-9)

Happy the mán who féars the Lórd,*
who tákes delíght in all his commánds.
His sóns will be pówerful on éarth;*
the children of the úpright are bléssed.

Ríches and wéalth are in his hóuse;*
his jústice stands fírm for éver.
He is a líght in the dárkness for the úpright:*
he is génerous, mérciful and júst.

The góod man takes píty and lénds,*
he condúcts his affáirs with hónour.
The júst man will néver wáver:*
hé will be remémbered for éver.

He has no féar of évil néws;*
with a fírm heart he trústs in the Lórd.
With a stéadfast héart he will not féar;*
he will sée the dównfall of his fóes.

Open-hánded, he gíves to the póor;†
his jústice stands fírm for éver.*
His héad will be ráised in glóry.

The wícked man sées and is ángry,†
grinds his téeth and fádes awáy;*
the desíre of the wicked leads to dóom.

Glory be to the Father . . .

Ant. Blessed are those who hunger and thirst for justice, for they shall have their fill.
Ant. 3: Praise God, all you his servants, both great and small, alleluia.

When chanted, the following canticle is sung with Alleluia *as set out. When recited, it suffices to say* Alleluia *at the beginning and end of each strophe.*

THE MARRIAGE FEAST OF THE LAMB   CANTICLE
                                      CF REVELATION 19:1-2, 5-7

Alleluia.
Salvation and glory and power belong to our God,*
(℟ Alleluia.)
His judgements are true and just.
℟ Alleluia (alleluia).

Alleluia.
Praise our God, all you his servants,*
(℟ Alleluia.)
You who fear him, small and great.
℟ Alleluia (alleluia).

Alleluia.
The Lord our God, the Almighty, reigns,*
(℟ Alleluia.)
Let us rejoice and exult and give him the glory.
℟ Alleluia (alleluia).

Alleluia.
The marriage of the Lamb has come,*
(℟ Alleluia).
And his bride has made herself ready.
℟ Alleluia (alleluia).

Ant. Praise God, all you his servants, both great and small, alleluia.

Scripture Reading   *Hebrews 12:22-24*
What you have come to is Mount Zion and the city of the living
God, the heavenly Jerusalem where the millions of angels have
gathered for the festival, with the whole Church in which everyone
is a "first-born son" and a citizen of heaven. You have come to
God himself, the supreme Judge, and been placed with spirits of
the saints who have been made perfect; and to Jesus, the mediator

who brings a new covenant and a blood for purification which
pleads more insistently than Abel's.

Short Responsory

Cantor: Great is our Lord; great is his might.
All: **Great is our Lord; great is his might.**
Cantor: His wisdom can never be measured.
All: **Great is our Lord; great is his might.**
Cantor: Glory be to the Father, and to the Son, and to the Holy
      Spirit.
All: **Great is our Lord; great is his might.**

Magnificat
The antiphon varies each week. See pp. 74ff.

My soul glorifies the Lord,*
my spirit rejoices in God, my Saviour.
He looks on his servant in her lowliness;*
henceforth all ages will call me blessed.

The Almighty works marvels for me.*
Holy his name!
His mercy is from age to age,*
on those who fear him.

He puts forth his arm in strength*
and scatters the proud-hearted.
He casts the mighty from their thrones*
and raises the lowly.

He fills the starving with good things,*
sends the rich away empty.

He protects Israel, his servant,*
remembering his mercy,
the mercy promised to our fathers,*
to Abraham and his sons for ever.

Glory be to the Father . . .

Repeat Magnificat antiphon.

Intercessions

In the Church, God has made known to us his hidden purpose: to make all things one in Christ. Let us pray that his will be done.

R̝. **Father, unite all things in Christ.**

We give you thanks for the presence and power of your Spirit in the Church:—give us the will to search for unity, and inspire us to pray and work together. R̝.

We give you thanks for all whose work proclaims your love:—help us to serve the communities in whose life we share. R̝.

Father, care for all who serve in the Church as ministers of your word and sacraments:—may they bring your whole family to the unity for which Christ prayed. R̝.

Your people have known the ravages of war and hatred:—grant that they may know the peace left by your Son. R̝.

Fulfil the hopes of those who sleep in your peace:—bring them to that final resurrection when you will be all in all. R̝.

Our Father

Concluding Prayer varies each week. See pp. 74ff.
Conclusion, as on p. 13.

Sundays 2-33 Through the Year
MAGNIFICAT ANTIPHONS AND CONCLUDING PRAYERS

SUNDAY 2

Magnificat ant. There was a wedding at Cana in Galilee, and Jesus was there with Mary his mother.

Concluding Prayer
Almighty God,
ruler of all things in heaven and on earth,
listen favourably to the prayer of your people,
and grant us your peace in our day.
(We make our prayer) through our Lord.

SUNDAY 3

Magnificat ant. The spirit of the Lord rests upon me; he has sent me to preach his Gospel to the poor.

Concluding Prayer
All-powerful, ever-living God,
direct our steps in the way of your love,
so that our whole life may be fragrant
with all we do in the name of Jesus, your beloved Son,
who lives and reigns with you and the Holy Spirit,
God, for ever and ever.

SUNDAY 4

Magnificat ant. Everyone was astonished at the words that came from the mouth of God.

Concluding Prayer
Lord our God,
make us love you above all things,
and all our fellow-men
with a love that is worthy of you.
(We make our prayer) through our Lord.

SUNDAY 5

Magnificat ant. Master, we have worked hard all night and have caught nothing; but if you say so, I will let down the nets.

Concluding Prayer
Guard your family, Lord, with constant loving care,
for in your divine grace we place our only hope.
(We make our prayer) through our Lord.

SUNDAY 6

Magnificat ant. Blessed are you who are in need; the kingdom of God is yours. Blessed are you who hunger now; you shall be satisfied.

Concluding Prayer
To those who love you, Lord,
you promise to come with your Son
and make your home within them.
Come then with your purifying grace
and make our hearts a place where you can dwell.
(We make our prayer) through our Lord.

SUNDAY 7
Magnificat ant. Do not judge, and you will not be judged, says the
Lord; as you judge others, so you also will be judged.

Concluding Prayer
Grant, almighty God,
that with our thoughts always on the things of the Spirit
we may please you in all that we say and do.
(We make our prayer) through our Lord.

SUNDAY 8
Magnificat ant. A good tree cannot bear bad fruit; a bad tree cannot
bring forth good fruit.

Concluding Prayer
In your mercy, Lord, direct the affairs of men so peaceably
that your Church may serve you in tranquillity and joy.
(We make our prayer) through our Lord.

SUNDAY 9
Magnificat ant. Lord, I am not worthy to have you under my roof;
only say the word and my servant will be healed.

Concluding Prayer
Lord God, by whom our lives are governed with unfailing wisdom
    and love,
take away from us all that is harmful
and give us all that will be for our good.
(We make our prayer) through our Lord.

SUNDAY 10

Magnificat ant. A great prophet has risen up among us and God has come to visit his people.

Concluding Prayer
Lord God, source of all good,
hear our prayer:
inspire us with good intentions,
and help us to fulfil them.
(We make our prayer) through our Lord.

SUNDAY 11

Magnificat ant. Jesus said to the woman, "Your faith has saved you. Go in peace."

Concluding Prayer
Lord God, strength of those who hope in you,
support us in our prayer:
because we are weak and can do nothing without you,
give us always the help of your grace
so that, in fulfilling your commandments,
we may please you in all we desire and do.
(We make our prayer) through our Lord.

SUNDAY 12

Magnificat ant. If any man wishes to come after me, he must deny himself and take up his cross, and in that way he must follow me.

Concluding Prayer
Lord God,
teach us at all times to fear and love your holy name,
for you never withdraw your guiding hand
for those you establish in your love.
(We make our prayer) through our Lord.

SUNDAY 13

Magnificat ant. The Son of Man came not to destroy souls but to save them.

Concluding Prayer
Lord God,
since by the adoption of grace,
you have made us children of light:
do not let false doctrine darken our minds,
but grant that your light may shine within us
and we may always live in the brightness of truth.
(We make our prayer) through our Lord.

SUNDAY 14
Magnificat ant. The harvest is great, but the labourers are few.
Pray to the Lord of the harvest that he may send labourers into his
harvest.

Concluding Prayer
Lord God,
when our world lay in ruins
you raised it up again
on the foundation of your Son's passion and death;
give us grace to rejoice in the freedom from sin
which he gained for us,
and bring us to everlasting joy.
(We make our prayer) through our Lord.

SUNDAY 15
Magnificat ant. "Master, what is the greatest commandment in the
Law?" Jesus said to him, "You must love the Lord your God with
all your heart, alleluia."

Concluding Prayer
God and Father,
to those who go astray you reveal the light of your truth
and enable them to return to the right path:
grant that all who have received the grace of baptism
may strive to be worthy of their Christian calling,
and reject everything opposed to it.
(We make our prayer) through our Lord.

SUNDAY 16

Magnificat ant. Mary has chosen the better part and it will never be taken from her.

Concluding Prayer
Be gracious, Lord, to us who serve you,
and in your kindness increase your gifts of grace within us:
so that fervent in faith, hope and love
we may be ever on the watch
and persevere in doing what you command.
(We make our prayer) through our Lord.

SUNDAY 17

Magnificat ant. Ask, and you will receive; seek, and you will find; knock, and the door will be opened to you, alleluia.

Concluding Prayer
Lord God, protector of those who hope in you,
without whom nothing is strong, nothing holy,
support us always with your love.
Guide us so to use the good things of this world,
that even now we may hold fast to what endures for ever.
(We make our prayer) through our Lord.

SUNDAY 18

Magnificat ant. If you wish to be truly rich, my brothers, then seek true riches.

Concluding Prayer
We recognise with joy
that you, Lord, created us,
and that you guide us by your providence.
In your unfailing kindness
support us in our prayer:
renew your life within us,
guard it and make it bear fruit for eternity.
(We make our prayer) through our Lord.

SUNDAY 19

Magnificat ant. Wherever your treasure is, there also will your heart be, says the Lord.

Concluding Prayer
Almighty, ever-living God,
we confidently call you Father as well as Lord.
Renew your Spirit in our hearts,
make us ever more perfectly your children,
so that we may enter upon the inheritance you have promised us.
(We make our prayer) through our Lord.

SUNDAY 20

Magnificat ant. I have come to spread a fire on earth, and how I wish it were blazing already.

Concluding Prayer
Lord God,
you have prepared for those who love you
what no eye has seen, no ear has heard.
Fill our hearts with your love,
so that loving you above all and in all,
we may attain your promises
which the heart of man has not conceived.
(We make our prayer) through our Lord.

SUNDAY 21

Magnificat ant. Many will come from the east and from the west to take their places with Abraham and Isaac and Jacob in the kingdom of heaven.

Concluding Prayer
Lord, by your grace we are made one in mind and heart.
Give us a love for what you command
and a longing for what you promise,
so that, amid this world's changes,
our hearts may be set on the world of lasting joy.
(We make our prayer) through our Lord.

SUNDAY 22

Magnificat ant. When you are invited to a marriage feast sit in the lowest place, so that the one who invited you can say to you, "Friend, take a higher place." Then everyone with you at table will see you honoured, alleluia.

Concluding Prayer
Father of might and power,
every good and perfect gift
comes down to us from you.
Implant in our hearts the love of your name,
increase our zeal for your service,
nourish what is good in us
and tend it with watchful care.
(We make our prayer) through our Lord.

SUNDAY 23

Magnificat ant. Whoever does not take up his cross and follow me, cannot be my disciple, says the Lord.

Concluding Prayer
Since it is from you, God our Father,
that redemption comes to us, your adopted children:
look with favour on the family you love,
give true freedom to us and to all who believe in Christ,
and bring us all alike to our eternal heritage.
(We make our prayer) through our Lord.

SUNDAY 24

Magnificat ant. I say to you that there is great joy among the angels when one sinner repents.

Concluding Prayer
Look upon us, Lord, creator and ruler of the whole world:
give us grace to serve you with all our heart
that we may come to know the power of your forgiveness and love.
(We make our prayer) through our Lord.

SUNDAY 25

Magnificat ant. No man can serve two masters. You cannot serve
both God and money.

Concluding Prayer
Father,
you summed up the whole law
as love of you and of our neighbour.
Grant that by keeping this commandment of love,
we may come to eternal life.
(We make our prayer) through our Lord.

SUNDAY 26

Magnificat ant. My son, remember that you received good things
during your life, just as Lazarus received bad things.

Concluding Prayer
Lord,
you reveal your mighty power
most of all by your forgiveness and compassion:
fill us constantly with your grace
as we hasten to share the joys you have promised us in heaven.
(We make our prayer) through our Lord.

SUNDAY 27

Magnificat ant. Say to yourselves, "We are useless servants, we
only did what we had to do."

Concluding Prayer
Almighty, ever-living God,
whose love surpasses all that we ask or deserve,
open up for us the treasures of your mercy.
Forgive us all that weighs on our conscience,
and grant us more even than we dare to ask.
(We make our prayer) through our Lord.

SUNDAY 28

Magnificat ant. When one of them saw that he had been made clean, he went back and gave praise to God with a loud voice, alleluia.

Concluding Prayer
Lord God,
open our hearts to your grace.
Let it go before us and be with us,
that we may always be intent upon doing your will.
(We make our prayer) through our Lord.

SUNDAY 29

Magnificat ant. When the Son of Man comes, do you think he will find faith on earth?

Concluding Prayer
Almighty, ever-living God,
make us ever obey you willingly and promptly.
Teach us how to serve you
with sincere and upright hearts
in every sphere of life.
(We make our prayer) through our Lord.

SUNDAY 30

Magnificat ant. The publican went home justified, for everyone who exalts himself will be humbled, but the man who humbles himself will be exalted.

Concluding Prayer
Lord God, deepen our faith,
strengthen our hope,
enkindle our love:
and so that we may obtain what you promise
make us love what you command.
(We make our prayer) through our Lord.

SUNDAY 31

Magnificat ant. The Son of Man came to seek out and to save that which was lost.

Concluding Prayer
God of power and mercy,
by whose grace your people give you praise and worthy service:
save us from faltering on our way
to the joys you have promised.
(We make our prayer) through our Lord.

SUNDAY 32

Magnificat ant. He is God, not of the dead, but of the living: because for him all things are alive, alleluia.

Concluding Prayer
Defend us, Lord, against every distress
so that unencumbered in body and soul,
we may devote ourselves to your service in freedom and joy.
(We make our prayer) through our Lord.

SUNDAY 33

Magnificat ant. Your endurance will win you your lives, says the Lord.

Concluding Prayer
Lord our God,
give us grace to serve you always with joy,
because our full and lasting happiness
is to make of our lives
a constant service to the Author of all that is good.
(We make our prayer) through our Lord.

PSALMS AND CANTICLES

Psalms

I

THE LORD IS THE KING OF ALL   PSALM 46(47)
*He is seated at the right hand of the Father, and his kingdom will have
no end*

All péoples, cláp your hánds,*
cry to Gód with shóuts of jóy!
For the Lórd, the Most Hígh, we must féar,*
great kíng over áll the éarth.

He subdúes péoples únder us*
and nátions únder our féet.
Our inhéritance, our glóry, is from hím,*
gíven to Jácob out of lóve.

God goes úp with shóuts of jóy;*
the Lord ascénds with trúmpet blást.
Sing práise for Gód, sing práise,*
sing práise to our kíng, sing práise.

God is kíng of áll the éarth,*
Sing práise with áll your skíll.
God is kíng óver the nátions;*
God réigns on his hóly thróne.

The prínces of the péoples are assémbled*
with the péople of Ábraham's Gód.
The rúlers of the éarth belong to Gód,*
to Gód who réigns over áll.

Glory be to the Father . . .

2
THE MESSIAH IS KING AND PRIEST   PSALM 109(110):1-5, 7
He must be king so that he may put all his enemies under his feet
(1 Corinthians 15:25)

The Lórd's revelátion to my Máster:†
"Sít on my ríght:*
your fóes I will pút beneath your féet."

The Lórd will wíeld from Síon†
your scéptre of pówer:*
rúle in the mídst of all your fóes.

A prínce from the dáy of your bírth†
on the hóly móuntains;*
from the wómb before the dáwn I begót you.

The Lórd has sworn an óath he will not chánge.†
"You are a príest for éver,*
a príest like Melchízedek of óld."

The Máster stánding at your ríght hand*
will shatter kíngs in the dáy of his wráth.

He shall drínk from the stréam by the wáyside*
and thérefore he shall líft up his héad.

Glory be to the Father . . .

GREAT ARE THE WORKS OF THE LORD   PSALM 110(111)
How great and wonderful are all your works, Lord God Almighty
Revelation 15:3)

I will thánk the Lórd with all my héart*
in the méeting of the júst and their assémbly.
Gréat are the wórks of the Lórd;*
to be póndered by áll who lóve them.

Majéstic and glórious his wórk,*
his jústice stands firm for éver.
He mákes us remémber his wónders.*
The Lórd is compássion and lóve.

He gives fóod to thóse who féar him;*
keeps his cóvenant éver in mínd.
He has shówn his míght to his péople*
by gíving them the lánds of the nátions.

His wórks are jústice and trúth:*
his précepts are áll of them súre,
standing firm for éver and éver:*
they are máde in úprightness and trúth.

He has sént delíverance to his péople†
and estáblished his cóvenant for éver.*
Hóly his náme, to be féared.

To fear the Lórd is the first stage of wísdom;†
all who dó so próve themselves wíse.*
His práise shall lást for éver!

Glory be to the Father . . .

4

THE HAPPINESS OF A JUST MAN   PSALM 111(112)

Be like children of the light; for the fruits of the light are seen in com-
plete goodness and right living and truth (Ephesians 5:8-9)

Happy the mán who féars the Lórd,*
who tákes delíght in all his commánds.
His sóns will be pówerful on éarth;*
the chíldren of the úpright are bléssed.

Ríches and wéalth are in his hóuse;*
his jústice stands fírm for éver.
He is a líght in the dárkness for the úpright:*
he is génerous, mérciful and júst.

The góod man takes píty and lénds,*
he condúcts his affáirs with hónour.
The júst man will néver wáver:*
hé will be remémbered for éver.

He has no féar of évil néws;*
with a fírm heart he trústs in the Lórd.
With a stéadfast héart he will not féar;*
he will sée the dównfall of his fóes.

Open-hánded, he gíves to the póor;†
his jústice stands fírm for éver.*
His héad will be ráised in glóry.

The wícked man sées and is ángry,†
grinds his téeth and fádes awáy;*
the desíre of the wícked leads to dóom.

Glory be to the Father . . .

5
PRAISED BE THE NAME OF THE LORD   PSALM 112(113)
He put down princes from their thrones and exalted the lowly (Luke
1:52)

Práise, O sérvants of the Lórd,*
práise the náme of the Lórd!
May the náme of the Lórd be bléssed*
both nów and for évermóre!
From the rísing of the sún to its sétting*
práised be the náme of the Lórd!

Hígh above all nátions is the Lórd,*
abóve the héavens his glóry.
Whó is like the Lórd, our Gód,*
who has rísen on hígh to his thróne
yet stóops from the héights to look dówn,*
to look dówn upon héaven and éarth?

From the dúst he lífts up the lówly,*
from his mísery he ráises the póor
to sét him in the cómpany of prínces,*
yés, with the prínces of his péople.
To the chíldless wife he gives a hóme*
and gláddens her héart with chíldren.

Glory be to the Father . . .

6

ISRAEL IS FREED FROM EGYPT   PSALM 113A(114):1-8
*You, who have renounced this world, have also been led forth from
Egypt* (St Augustine)

When Ísrael came fórth from Égypt,*
Jacob's sóns from an álien péople,
Júdah becáme the Lord's témple,*
Ísrael becáme his kíngdom.

The séa fléd at the síght:*
the Jórdan turned báck on its cóurse,
the móuntains léapt like ráms*
and the hílls like yéarling shéep.

Whý was it, séa, that you fléd,*
that you túrned back, Jórdan, on your cóurse?
Móuntains, that you léapt like ráms,*
hílls, like yéarling shéep?

Trémble, O éarth, before the Lórd,*
in the présence of the Gód of Jácob,
who túrns the róck into a póol*
and flínt into a spríng of wáter.

Glory be to the Father . . .

7

PRAISE OF THE GOD OF TRUTH   PSALM 113B(115)
Turn away from idols and worship the living and true God (1 Thessalonians 1:9)

Not to ús, Lórd, not to ús,*
but to yóur náme give the glóry
for the sáke of your lóve and your trúth,*
lest the héathen say: "Whére is their Gód?"

But our Gód is ín the héavens;*
he dóes whatéver he wílls.

Their ídols are sílver and góld,*
the wórk of húman hánds.

They have móuths but they cánnot spéak;*
they have éyes but they cánnot sée;
they have éars but they cánnot héar;*
they have nóstrils but they cánnot sméll.

With their hánds they cánnot féel;†
with their féet they cánnot wálk.*
No sóund cómes from their thróats.
Their mákers will cóme to be líke them*
and so will áll who trúst in thém.

Sons of Ísrael, trúst in the Lórd;*
hé is their hélp and their shíeld.
Sons of Áaron, trúst in the Lórd;*
hé is their hélp and their shíeld.

You who féar him, trúst in the Lórd;*
hé is their hélp and their shíeld.
He remémbers us, and hé will bléss us;†
he will bléss the sóns of Ísrael.*
He will bléss the sóns of Áaron.

The Lord will bléss thóse who féar him,*
the líttle no léss than the gréat:
to yoú may the Lórd grant íncrease,*
to yóu and áll your chíldren.

May yóu be bléssed by the Lórd,*
the máker of héaven and éarth.
The héavens belóng to the Lórd*
but the éarth he has gíven to mén.

The déad shall not práise the Lórd,*
nor thóse who go dówn into the sílence.
But wé who líve bless the Lórd*
nów and for éver. Amén.

Glory be to the Father . . .

8
THANKSGIVING IN THE TEMPLE   PSALM 115(116)
Through him (Christ), let us offer God an unending sacrifice of praise
(Hebrews 13:15)

I trústed, éven when I sáid:*
"I am sórely afflícted,"
and whén I sáid in my alárm:*
"No mán can be trústed."

How cán I repáy the Lórd*
for his góodness to mé?
The cúp of salvátion I will ráise;*
I will cáll on the Lórd's name.

My vóws to the Lórd I will fulfíl*
befóre all his péople.
O précious in the éyes of the Lórd*
is the déath of his fáithful.

Your sérvant, Lord, your sérvant am Í;*
you have lóosened my bónds.
A thánksgiving sácrifice I máke:*
I will cáll on the Lórd's name.

My vóws to the Lórd I will fulfíl*
befóre all his péople,
in the cóurts of the hóuse of the Lórd,*
in your mídst, O Jerúsalem.

Glory be to the Father . . .

9
GOD, THE PROTECTOR OF HIS PEOPLE   PSALM 120(121)
*They will never hunger or thirst again; neither the sun nor scorching
wind will ever plague them* (Revelation 7:16)

I líft up my éyes to the móuntains:*
from whére shall come my hélp?
My hélp shall cóme from the Lórd*
who made héaven and éarth.

May he néver állow you to stúmble!*
Let him sléep not, your guárd.
Nó, he sléeps not nor slúmbers,*
Israel's guárd.

The Lórd is your guárd and your sháde;*
at your ríght side he stánds.
By dáy the sún shall not smíte you*
nor the móon in the níght.

The Lórd will guárd you from évil,*
he will guárd your sóul.
The Lord will guárd your góing and cóming*
both nów and for éver.

Glory be to the Father . . .

10
THE HOLY CITY OF JERUSALEM   PSALM 121(122)
You have come to Mount Zion and the city of the living God, the heavenly Jerusalem (Hebrews 12:22)

I rejóiced when I héard them sáy:*
"Let us gó to God's hóuse."
And nów our féet are stánding*
within your gátes, O Jerúsalem.

Jerúsalem is búilt as a cíty*
stróngly compáct.
It is thére that the tríbes go úp,*
the tríbes of the Lórd.

For Ísrael's láw it ís,*
there to práise the Lord's náme.
Thére were set the thrónes of júdgement*
of the hóuse of Dávid.

For the péace of Jerúsalem práy:*
"Péace be to your hómes!
May péace réign in your wálls,*
in your pálaces, péace!"

For lóve of my bréthren and fríends*
I say: "Péace upon yóu!"
For lóve of the hóuse of the Lórd*
I will ásk for your góod.

Glory be to the Father . . .

II
SUCCESS DEPENDS ON THE LORD'S BLESSING
You are God's building (1 Corinthians 3:9)

If the Lórd does not buíld the hóuse,*
in váin do its buílders lábour;
if the Lórd does not wátch over the cíty,*
in váin does the wátchman keep vígil.

In váin is your éarlier rísing,*
your góing láter to rést,
you who tóil for the bréad you éat:*
when he pours gífts on his belóved while they slúmber.

Truly sóns are a gíft from the Lórd,*
a bléssing, the frúit of the wómb.
Indéed the sóns of yóuth*
are like árrows in the hánd of a wárrior.

Ó the háppiness of the mán*
who has fílled his quíver with these árrows!
Hé will have no cáuse for sháme*
when he dispútes with his fóes in the gáteways.

Glory be to the Father . . .

12
OUT OF THE DEPTHS I CRY   PSALM 129(130)
He will save his people from their sins (Matthew 1:21)

Out of the dépths I crý to you, O Lórd,*
†Lórd, hear my vóice!
O lét your éars be atténtive*
to the vóice of my pléading.

If you, O Lórd, should márk our guílt,*
Lórd, who would survíve?
But with yóu is fóund forgíveness:*
for thís we revére you.

My sóul is wáiting for the Lórd,*
I cóunt on his wórd.
My sóul is lónging for the Lórd*
more than wátchman for dáybreak.
Let the wátchman cóunt on dáybreak*
and Ísrael on the Lórd.

Becáuse with the Lórd there is mércy*
and fúlness of redémption,
Ísrael indéed he will redéem*
from áll its iníquity.

Glory be to the Father . . .

13
PRAISE OF GOD'S MAJESTY   PSALM 144(145); 1-13
You, O Lord, are the One who was and who is, the Just One (Revelation 16:5)

I will give you glóry, O Gód my Kíng,*
I will bléss your náme for éver.

I will bléss you dáy after dáy*
and práise your náme for éver.
The Lord is gréat, híghly to be práised,*
his gréatness cánnot be méasured.

Age to áge shall procláim your wórks,*
shall decláre your míghty déeds,
shall spéak of your spléndour and glóry,*
tell the tále of your wónderful wórks.

They will spéak of your térrible déeds,*
recóunt your gréatness and míght.
They will recáll your abúndant góodness;*
age to áge shall ríng out your jústice.

The Lord is kínd and fúll of compássion,*
slow to ánger, abóunding in lóve.
How góod is the Lórd to áll,*
compássionate to áll his créatures.

All your créatures shall thánk you, O Lórd,*
and your fríends shall repéat their bléssing.
They shall spéak of the glóry of your réign*
and decláre your míght, O Gód,
to make knówn to mén your mighty déeds*
and the glórious spléndour of your réign.
Yóurs is an éverlasting kíngdom;*
your rúle lasts from áge to áge.

Glory be to the Father . . .

14
THE RENEWAL OF JERUSALEM   PSALM 147
Come, and I will show you the bride that the Lamb has chosen (Revelation 21:9)

O práise the Lórd, Jerúsalem!*
†Síon, práise your Gód!

He has stréngthened the bárs of your gátes,*
he has bléssed the chíldren withín you.
He éstablished péace on your bórders,*
he féeds you with fínest whéat.

He sénds out his wórd to the éarth*
and swíftly rúns his commánd.
He shówers down snów white as wóol,*
he scátters hóar-frost like áshes.

He húrls down háilstones like crúmbs.*
The wáters are frózen at his tóuch;
he sénds forth his wórd and it mélts them:*
at the bréath of his móuth the waters flów.

He mákes his wórd known to Jácob,*
to Ísrael his láws and decrées.
He has not déalt thus with óther nátions;*
he has not táught them hís decrées.

Glory be to the Father . . .

Canticles

15
GOD, THE SAVIOUR   CANTICLE: EPHESIANS 1:3-10

Blessed be the God and Father*
of our Lord Jesus Christ,
who has blessed us in Christ*
with every spiritual blessing in the heavenly places.

He chose us in him*
before the foundation of the world,
that we should be holy*
and blameless before him.

He destined us in love*
to be his sons through Jesus Christ,
according to the purpose of his will,†
to the praise of his glorious grace*
which he freely bestowed on us in the Beloved.

In him we have redemption through his blood,*
the forgiveness of our trespasses,
according to the riches of his grace*
which he lavished upon us.

He has made known to us†
in all wisdom and insight*
the mystery of his will,
according to his purpose*
which he set forth in Christ.

His purpose he set forth in Christ,*
as a plan for the fulness of time,
to unite all things in him,*
things in heaven and things on earth.

Glory be to the Father . . .

16
CHRIST, THE SERVANT OF GOD   CANTICLE: PHILIPPIANS 2:6-11

Though he was in the form of God,*
Jesus did not count equality with God a thing to be grasped.

He emptied himself,†
taking the form of a servant,*
being born in the likeness of men.

And being found in human form,†
he humbled himself and became obedient unto death,*
even death on a cross.

Therefore God has highly exalted him*
and bestowed on him the name which is above every name,

That at the name of Jesus every knee should bow,*
in heaven and on earth and under the earth,

And every tongue confess that Jesus Christ is Lord,*
to the glory of God the Father.

Glory be to the Father . . .

17
CHRIST IS THE FIRSTBORN OF ALL CREATION,   CANTICLE
THE FIRSTBORN FROM THE DEAD   COLOSSIANS 1:12-20

Let us give thanks to the Father,†
who has qualified us to share*
in the inheritance of the saints in light.

He has delivered us from the dominion of darkness*
and transferred us to the kingdom of his beloved Son,
in whom we have redemption,*
the forgiveness of sins.

He is the image of the invisible God,*
the firstborn of all creation,
for in him all things were created, in heaven and on earth,
visible and invisible.

All things were created*
through him and for him.
He is before all things,*
and in him all things hold together.

He is the head of the body, the Church;*
he is the beginning,
the firstborn from the dead,*
that in everything he might be pre-eminent.

For in him all the fulness of God was pleased to dwell,*
and through him to reconcile to himself all things,
whether on earth or in heaven,*
making peace by the blood of his cross.

Glory be to the Father . . .

18
CHRIST, THE SERVANT OF GOD,   CANTICLE
FREELY ACCEPTS HIS PASSION   I PETER 2:21-24

Christ suffered for you,†
leaving you an example*
that you should follow in his steps.

He committed no sin;*
no guile was found on his lips.
When he was reviled,*
he did not revile in return.

When he suffered,*
he did not threaten;
but he trusted to him*
who judges justly.

He himself bore our sins*
in his body on the tree,
that we might die to sin*
and live to righteousness.

By his wounds you have been healed.

Glory be to the Father . . .

19
THE JUDGEMENT OF GOD   CANTICLE
                                    REVELATION 11:17-18; 12:10b-12a

We give thanks to you, Lord God Almighty,*
who are and who were,
that you have taken your great power*
and begun to reign.

The nations raged,*
but your wrath came,
and the time for the dead to be judged,*
for rewarding your servants, the prophets and saints,
and those who fear your name,*
both small and great.

Now the salvation and the power†
and the kingdom of our God*
and the authority of his Christ have come,
for the accuser of our brethren has been thrown down,*
who accuses them day and night before our God.

And they have conquered him*
by the blood of the Lamb
and by the word of their testimony,*
for they loved not their lives even unto death.
Rejoice, then, O heaven,*
and you that dwell therein.

Glory be to the Father . . .

20
HYMN OF ADORATION   CANTICLE: REVELATION 15:3-4

Great and wonderful are your deeds,*
O Lord God the Almighty!
Just and true are your ways,*
O King of the ages!

Who shall not fear and glorify your name, O Lord?*
For you alone are holy.
All nations shall come and worship you,*
for your judgements have been revealed.

Glory be to the Father . . .

21

When chanted, this canticle is sung with Alleluia *as set out below.
When recited, it suffices to say* Alleluia *at the beginning and end of
each strophe.*

THE MARRIAGE FEAST OF THE LAMB   CANTICLE
                                    CF REVELATION 19: 1-2, 5-7

Alleluia.
Salvation and glory and power belong to our God,*
(℞ Alleluia.)
His judgements are true and just.
℞ Alleluia (alleluia).

Alleluia.
Praise our God, all you his servants,*
(℞ Alleluia.)
You who fear him, small and great.
℞ Alleluia (alleluia).

Alleluia.
The Lord our God, the Almighty, reigns,*
(℞ Alleluia.)
Let us rejoice and exult and give him the glory.
℞ Alleluia (alleluia).

Alleluia.
The marriage of the Lamb has come,*
(℞ Alleluia.)
And his bride has made herself ready.
℞ Alleluia (alleluia).

Glory be to the Father . . .

22
MAGNIFICAT   CANTICLE: LUKE I: 45-55

My soul glorifies the Lord,*
my spirit rejoices in God, my saviour.
He looks on his servant in her lowliness;*
henceforth all ages will call me blessed.

The Almighty works marvels for me.*
Holy his name!
His mercy is from age to age,*
on those who fear him.

He puts forth his arm in strength*
and scatters the proud-hearted.
He casts the mighty from their thrones*
and raises the lowly.

He fills the starving with good things,*
sends the rich away empty.

He protects Israel, his servant,*
remembering his mercy,
the mercy promised to our fathers,*
to Abraham and his sons for ever.

Glory be to the Father . . .

Alternative version, see p. 123.

HYMNS

The hymns given in this book are a selection from those recommended for use in Evening Prayer from The Divine Office. *Any other hymn approved by the local Episcopal Conference may be substituted provided it is suitable for the hour, the season, or the feast (cf. General Instruction n. 178.)*

Advent

23
O come, O come, Emmanuel,
And ransom captive Israel,
That mourns in lonely exile here
Until the Son of God appear.
   Rejoice! Rejoice! Emmanuel
   Shall come to you, O Israel!

O come, now Wisdom from on high,
Who orders all things mightily;
To us the path of knowledge show,
and teach us in her ways to go.
   Rejoice! etc. . . .

O come, O come, now Lord of might,
Who to your tribes on Sinai's height
In ancient times you gave the law,
In cloud, and majesty, and awe.
   Rejoice! etc. . . .

24

O come, now Rod of Jesse's stem,
From every foe deliver them
That trust your mighty power to save,
And give them vict'ry o'er the grave.
   Rejoice! Rejoice! Emmanuel
   Shall come to you, O Israel!

O come, now Key of David, come,
And open wide our heav'nly home;
Make safe the way that leads on high,
And close the path to misery.
   Rejoice! etc. . . . .

O come, now Day-spring from on high,
And cheer us by your drawing nigh;
Disperse the gloomy clouds of night,
And death's dark shadow put to flight.
   Rejoice! etc. . . . .

O come, Desire of nations, bind
In one the hearts of all mankind;
Bid now our sad divisions cease,
And be yourself our King of Peace.
   Rejoice! etc. . . . .

Tr Thomas Helmore 1811-90

Hymns 23 and 24 may be joined to form one.

Christmastide I

25
O come, all ye faithful,
Joyful and triumphant,
O come ye, O come ye to Bethlehem;
Come and behold him
Born the King of Angels.
   O come, let us adore him,
   O come, let us adore him,
   O come, let us adore him, Christ the Lord.

God of God,
Light of Light,
Lo! he abhors not the virgin's womb;
Very God,
Begotten, not created.
   O come let us adore him, etc. . . .

Sing, choirs of angels,
Sing in exultation,
Sing, all ye citizens of heaven above;
"Glory to God
In the highest."
   O come let us adore him, etc. . . .

Yea, Lord we greet thee,
Born this happy morning,
Jesu, to thee be glory given;
Word of the Father
Now in flesh appearing.
   O come, let us adore him, etc. . . .

18th century
Tr F. Oakley 1802-80

26

Of the Father's love begotten,
Ere the worlds began to be,
He is Alpha and Omega,
He the source, the ending he,
Of all things that are and have been
And that future years shall see:
Evermore and evermore.

Blessèd was the day for ever
When the Virgin, full of grace,
By the Holy Ghost conceiving,
Bore the Saviour of our race,
And the child, the world's Redeemer,
First revealed his sacred face:
Evermore and evermore.

Glory be to God the Father,
Glory be to God the Son,
Glory to the Holy Spirit,
Persons three, yet Godhead one.
Glory be from all creation
While eternal ages run:
Evermore and evermore.

Aurelius C. Prudentius 348-*c.* 413
Tr J. M. Neale 1818-66
H. W. Baker 1821–77, and editors of *Praise The Lord* revised
(verse 3).

Christmastide II

27

Bethlehem, of noblest cities
None can once with thee compare:
Thou alone the Lord from heaven
Didst for us incarnate bear.

Fairer than the sun at morning
Was the star that told his birth;
To the lands their God announcing,
Seen in human form on earth.

By its peerless beauty guided
See the eastern kings appear;
Bowing low, their gifts they offer,
Gifts of incense, gold and myrrh.

Sacred gifts of mystic meaning:
Incense doth the God disclose,
Gold the King of Kings proclaimeth,
Myrrh a future tomb foreshows.

In thy glory, O Lord Jesus,
To the Gentile world displayed,
With the Father and the Spirit
Endless praise to thee be paid.

Aurelius C. Prudentius 348-c 413
Tr E. Caswall 1814-78 *and others*

28

Songs of thankfulness and praise,
Jesu, Lord, to thee we raise,
Manifested by the star
To the sages from afar;
Branch of royal David's stem
In thy birth at Bethlehem;
Anthems be to thee addressed,
God in man made manifest.

Manifest at Jordan's stream,
Prophet, priest and king supreme;
And at Cana wedding-guest
In thy Godhead manifest;
Manifest in power divine,
Changing water into wine;
Anthems be to thee addressed,
God in man made manifest.

Grant us grace to see thee, Lord,
Mirrored in thy holy word;
May we imitate thee now,
And be pure, as pure art thou;
That we like to thee may be
At thy great Epiphany,
And may praise thee, ever blest,
God in man made manifest.

C. Wordsworth 1807-85

Lent

29
God, of thy pity, unto us thy children
Bend down thy ear in thine own loving kindness,
And all thy people's prayers and vows ascending,
Hear, we beseech thee.

Look down in mercy from thy seat of glory,
Pour on our souls the radiance of thy presence,
Drive from our weary hearts the shades of darkness,
Lightening our footsteps.

Free us from sin by might of thy great loving,
Cleanse thou the sordid, loose the fettered spirit,
Spare every sinner, raise with thine own right hand,
All who are fallen.

Glory to God the Father everlasting,
Glory for ever to the Sole-begotten,
With whom thy Holy Spirit through the ages
Reigneth co-equal.

Ante-Tridentine Breviary
Tr Alan G. McDougall 1895-1964

30
Lord Jesus, think on me
And purge away my sins;
From earth-born passions set me free,
And make me pure within.

Lord Jesus, think on me,
With care and woe oppressed;
Let me thy loving servant be,
And taste thy promised rest.

Lord Jesus, think on me
Amid the battle's strife;
In all my pain and misery
Be thou my health and life.

Lord Jesus, think on me,
Nor let me go astray;
Through darkness and perplexity
Point thou the heavenly way.

Bishop Synesius 375-430

Holy Week

31
My song is love unknown,
My Saviour's love to me,
Love to the loveless shown,
That they might lovely be.
O who am I,
That for my sake
My Lord should take
Frail flesh and die?

Sometimes they strew his way
And his sweet praises sing;
Resounding all the day
Hosannas to their King;
Then "Crucify!"
Is all their breath,
And for his death
They thirst and cry.

They rise, and needs will have
My dear Lord made away;
A murderer they save,
The Prince of life they slay.
Yet cheerful he
To suffering goes,
That he his foes
From thence might free.

S. Crossman 1624-83

Eastertide I: Before Ascension Day

32
Christ the Lord is risen again!
Christ hath broken every chain,
Hark, the angels shout for joy,
Singing evermore on high,

Alleluya!

He who gave for us his life,
Who for us endured the strife,
Is our Paschal Lamb today!
We too sing for joy, and say

Alleluya!

He who bore all pain and loss
Comfortless upon the Cross,
Lives in glory now on high,
Pleads for us, and hears our cry.

Alleluya!

Now he bids us tell abroad
How the lost may be restored,
How the penitent forgiven,
How we too may enter heaven.

Alleluya!

Michael Weisse c. 1480-1534
Tr C. Winkworth 1829-78

33
Easter glory fills the sky! Alleluia!
Christ now lives, no more to die! Alleluia!
Darkness has been put to flight, Alleluia!
By the living Lord of light! Alleluia!

Mary, Mother, greet your Son,
Radiant from his triumph won!
By his cross you shared his pain,
So for ever share his reign!

Shepherd, seek the sheep that strayed!
Come to contrite Peter's aid!
Strengthen him to be the rock;
Make him shepherd of your flock!

Seek not life within the tomb;
Christ stands in the upper room!
Risen glory he conceals,
Risen body he reveals!

Though we see his face no more,
He is with us as before!
Glory veiled, he is our priest,
His true flesh and blood our feast!

James Quinn SJ

34
Alleluia, sing to Jesus, his the sceptre, his the throne.
Alleluia, his the triumph, his the victory alone.
Hark, the songs of holy Sion thunder like a mighty flood:
Jesus out of every nation hath redeemed us by his blood.

Alleluia, not as orphans are we left in sorrow now;
Alleluia, he is near us, faith believes nor questions how.
Though the clouds from sight received him when the forty days
    were o'er,
Shall our hearts forget his promise: "I am with you evermore"?
S. S. Wesley 1810-76

Eastertide II: After Ascension Day

35

Come, Holy Ghost, Creator, come
From thy bright heavenly throne,
Come, take possession of our souls,
And make them all thy own.

Thou who art called the Paraclete,
Best gift of God above,
The living spring, the living fire,
Sweet unction and true love.

Thou who art sev'nfold in thy grace,
Finger of God's right hand;
His promise, teaching little ones
To speak and understand.

O guide our minds with thy blest light,
With love our hearts inflame;
And with thy strength, which ne'er decays,
Confirm our mortal frame.

Far from us drive our deadly foe;
True peace unto us bring;
And through all perils lead us safe
Beneath thy sacred wing.

Through thee may we the Father know,
Through thee th'eternal Son,
And thee the Spirit of them both,
Thrice-blessed Three in One.

All glory to the Father be,
With his co-equal Son:
The same to thee, great Paraclete,
While endless ages run.

Attr to Rabanus Maurus 766-856
Tr Anon

36
Come down, O love divine,
Seek thou this soul of mine,
And visit it with thine own ardour glowing;
O Comforter draw near,
Within my heart appear,
And kindle it, thy holy flame bestowing.

O let it freely burn,
Till earthly passions turn
To dust and ashes in its heat consuming;
And let thy glorious light
Shine ever on my sight,
And clothe me round, the while my path illuming.

Let holy charity
Mine outward vesture be,
And lowliness become mine inner clothing.
True lowliness of heart,
Which takes the humbler part,
And o'er its own shortcomings weeps with loathing.

And so the yearning strong,
With which the soul will long,
Shall far outpass the power of human telling;
For none can guess its grace,
Till he become the place
Wherein the Holy Spirit makes his dwelling.

Bianco da Siena d 1434
Tr R. F. Littledale 1833-90

Through the Year

37
Praise to the holiest in the height,
And in the depth be praise,
In all his words most wonderful,
Most sure in all his ways.

O loving wisdom of our God!
When all was sin and shame,
A second Adam to the fight
And to the rescue came.

O wisest love! that flesh and blood
Which did in Adam fail,
Should strive afresh against their foe,
Should strive and should prevail.

And that a higher gift than grace
Should flesh and blood refine,
God's presence and his very self,
And essence all divine.

O generous love! that he who smote
In man for man the foe,
The double agony in man
For man should undergo.

J. H. Newman 1801-90

38

Holy God, we praise thy name;
Lord of all, we bow before thee!
All on earth thy sceptre own,
All in heaven above adore thee.
Infinite thy vast domain,
Everlasting is thy reign.

Hark! the loud celestial hymn,
Angel choirs above are raising;
Cherubim and seraphim,
In unceasing chorus praising,
Fill the heavens with sweet accord:
Holy, holy, holy, Lord.

Holy Father, holy Son,
Holy Spirit, three we name thee.
While in essence only one
Undivided God we claim thee;
And adoring bend the knee,
While we own the mystery.

Spare thy people, Lord, we pray,
By a thousand snares surrounded;
Keep us without sin today;
Never let us be confounded.
Lo, I put my trust in thee;
Never, Lord, abandon me.

C. A. Walworth 1820-1900

39
Praise, my soul, the King of heaven;
To his feet your tribute bring;
Ransomed, healed, restored, forgiven,
Who like me his praise should sing?
Praise him! Praise him!
Praise him! Praise him!
Praise the everlasting King.

Praise him for his grace and favour,
To our fathers in distress;
Praise him still the same for ever,
Slow to chide and swift to bless,
Praise him! Praise him!
Praise him! Praise him!
Glorious in his faithfulness.

Fatherlike, he tends and spares us;
Well our feeble frame he knows;
In his hands he gently bears us,
Rescues us from all our foes.
Praise him! Praise him!
Praise him! Praise him!
Widely as his mercy flows.

Angels, help us to adore him;
Ye behold him face to face;
Sun and moon bow down before him,
Dwellers all in time and space.
Praise him! Praise him!
Praise him! Praise him!
Praise with us the God of grace.

A. F. Lyte 1793-1847

Holy Trinity

40

Firmly I believe and truly
God is Three, and God is One;
And I next acknowledge duly
Manhood taken by the Son;

And I trust and hope most fully
In that manhood crucified;
And each thought and deed unruly
Do to death, as he has died.

Simply to his grace and wholly
Light and life and strength belong;
And I love supremely, solely,
Him the holy, him the strong.

Adoration aye be given,
With and through the angelic host,
To the God of earth and heaven,
Father, Son and Holy Ghost.

J. H. Newman 1801-90

Christ the King

41

Hail Redeemer, King divine!
Priest and Lamb, the throne is thine,
King, whose reign shall never cease,
Prince of everlasting peace.
  Angels, saints and nations sing
  "Praised be Jesus Christ, our King;
  Lord of life, earth, sky and sea,
  King of love on Calvary."

King, whose name creation thrills,
Rule our minds, our hearts, our wills,
Till in peace each nation rings
With thy praises, King of kings.
  Angels, etc. . . .

King most holy, King of truth,
Guide the lowly, guide the youth;
Christ, thou King of glory bright,
Be to us eternal light.
  Angels, etc. . . .

Shepherd-King o'er mountains steep
Homeward bring the wandering sheep;
Shelter in one royal fold
States and kingdoms, new and old.
  Angels, etc. . . .

Patrick Brennan

ALTERNATIVE TEXTS

The Canticle of Mary (Magnificat)

My soul proclaims the greatness of the Lord,*
my spirit rejoices in God my Saviour;
for he has looked with favour on his lowly servant,*
and from this day all generations will call me blessed.

The Almighty has done great things for me:*
holy is his Name.
He has mercy on those who fear him*
in every generation.

He has shown the strength of his arm,*
he has scattered the proud in their conceit.
He has cast down the mighty from their thrones,*
and has lifted up the lowly.
He has filled the hungry with good things,*
and has sent the rich away empty.

He has come to the help of his servant Israel*
for he has remembered his promise of mercy,
the promise he made to our fathers,*
to Abraham and his children for ever.

Glory to the Father, and to the Son, and to the Holy Spirit:
as in the beginning, so now, and for ever. Amen.

ICET translation

Introductions to the Our Father

1

Let us now pray to the Father, in the words our Saviour gave us: *Our Father* . . .

2

As we look to the coming of God's kingdom, let us say: *Our Father* . . .

3

Let us sum up our praise and petitions in the words of Christ, saying: *Our Father* . . .

4

Let us give a sure foundation to our praise and petitions by the Lord's Prayer: *Our Father* . . .

5

Let us, once more, praise the Father and pray to him in the words of Christ himself, saying: *Our Father* . . .

6

(Addressed to Christ) Lord, remember us in your kingdom, as following your teaching we say: *Our Father* . . .

7

Following our Lord's teaching, let us say with faith and trust: *Our Father* . . .

8

Let us fulfil our Lord's instruction, and say: *Our Father* . . .

9

Let us now together say those words which the Lord gave us as the pattern of all prayer: *Our Father* . . .

ACKNOWLEDGEMENTS

The publishers gratefully acknowledge permission to reproduce the following copyright material:

SCRIPTURE TEXTS

Jerusalem Bible, published and © 1966, 1967, 1968 by Darton, Longman & Todd Ltd, and Doubleday & Company Inc.: for 1 Corinthians 9:24-25; 11:23-25; 15:3-5, 8; 15:55-57; Galatians 4:4-5; Philippians 2:6-7; 2 Thessalonians 2:13-14; Hebrews 10:12-14; 12:22-24; 1 Peter 1:3-5; 3:18, 22; 1 John 1:1-3; Revelation 21:2-3, 22, 27

Knox Bible, © 1945, 1949, the Hierarchy of England and Wales, for Romans 5:20-21; 8:16-17.

Revised Standard Version, Common Bible, copyrighted © 1973, by the Division of Christian Education, National Council of the Churches of Christ in the USA. Special permission has been obtained to use in this publication the "you-your-yours" forms of the personal pronoun in the address to God. For the New Testament Canticles, Ephesians 1:3-10; Philippians 2:6-11; Colossians 1:12-20; 1 Timothy 3:16; 1 Peter 2:21-24; Revelation 4:11; 5:9, 10, 12; 11:17-18; 12:10b-12a; 15:3-4; 19:1-2, 5-7; and for Philippians 4:4-5.

Today's English Version (Good News for Modern Man), United Bible Societies of America, and Collins Publishers, London, for Acts 10:37-38; 13:23-25; 13:26-30a; 1 Corinthians 1:23-24; 2 Corinthians 1:3-4; Ephesians 2:4-7; 4:3-6; Titus 3:4-5.

Psalm texts are translated from the Hebrew by The Grail, © The Grail (England) 1963, and published by Collins in Fontana Books. They are reprinted from the Singing Version first published in Fontana Books in 1966. The practical needs of choral recitation prompted a number of revisions in the psalms, and these were made with the agreement of The Grail.

The Magnificat is given both in the version translated by The Grail, and in the version © 1970, 1971, International Consultation on English Texts.

HYMNS
Geoffrey Chapman Publishers, for James Quinn SJ, from *New Hymns for All Seasons*, no. 33, for editors of *Praise the Lord* revised, no. 26, verse 3.
Search Press, for nn. 29, 41.